Atomic Power With God Thru Fasting And Prayer

Franklin Hall

We have been able to conduct Healing Campaigns already in over a dozen of our states and on the island of Jamaica, B. W. I. In a single campaign which we conducted, as many as one hundred and twenty-five deaf-mutes, ninety totally blind, and hundreds of other equally miraculous deliverances have resulted. Happy and joyful conversions have numbered as many as nine thousand in one revival.

We found people all over the island acquainted with your books and tracts. Many were fasting and praying for this revival before we came.

Brother Hall, we wanted you to know, we do appreciate your vision, and the tremendous way you have STIRRED THE WORLD with FASTING AND PRAYER. We shall do all we can to push that part of the Gospel. We are going to handle your books in our meetings and shall order them in large quantities. You may send me one thousand of your, "Because of Your Unbelief," revival booklets.

Yours in Christ for the DELIVERANCE OF ALL,

T. L. OSBORN

Box 4231, Tulsa 9, Oklahoma.

SOUTH AFRICA
From Missionary Department

Administrative Offices
7 De Villiers Street
Johannesburg, South Africa

Beloved Brother in Christ:

Your books have been a real blessing and inspiration to my soul, and many are already testifying of great blessings that they received through the reading of your books and practicing protracted fasts. God has graciously helped me to complete a 24-day fast, with much blessing and a new revelation for His work.

The message God has given you in your books has come in these closing days of time to do a great work for Him. I want to encourage you to go on with the job.

My mission called for a mission-wide fast for 21 days, and on one Sunday during that time about 60,000 people were fasting and praying. Many went the full length and fasted for 21 days and even longer.

We have testimonies of wonderful healings. One young man was released from a leper institution, perfectly healed. Another child who was paralyzed, received healing and can now walk. Another was healed of T.B. of the bone; another of stomach cancer; another, who was involved in a motor accident and was unconscious for 18 days, was healed and is now one hundred percent well. There are other oustanding healings coming in daily, that are too numerous to mention. Many are now in a healing ministry.

We have noticed reports from all over this continent that a revival tidal wave is coming about through fasting and prayer. We give Christ the glory.

With warmest Christian greetings,
Yours in His Royal Service,
F. J. Hawley, Missionary Superintendent.

AUSTRALIA-NEW ZEALAND and AFRICA

Greetings to you in the Name of the Lord!

As you will see by this letterhead, I am the Australian secretary of the Russian and Eastern European Mission, and by the magazine forwarded under separate cover, the editor of an Australian magazine called, "The Evidence." Mr. Charles R. Bilby is manager of our New Zealand office, and they have been in touch with you in connection with your books.

Your books and literature on prayer and fasting have helped me a great deal. Recently I took a 23-day fast.

In addition to this fast, the last eleven campaigns in South Africa and Rhodesia, I have started with a call to the people to fast and pray. The response to this appeal has been most encouraging, and the mighty blessings experienced as a result of the fasting have been remarkable. Eight of these campaigns were started with a three-day fast, and the other three with a two-day fast.

I would prefer a long fast instead of many short fasts, but as these campaigns are for a week only, I have felt I was accomplishing more by speaking to new people each week and getting them to fast with me. It has all been very wonderful. Three days of fasting each week is about as much as one can manage.

Fasting in AFRICA has been given a great deal of emphasis in behalf of an international revival. *Brother Hawley*, the missionary Superintendent of the Apostolic Faith Mission, from whom you have received letters, and who has distributed a great number of your books, has done a great deal in this respect.

He recently took a 24-day fast. A letter yesterday from his assistant, Brother Eric Wilson, tells me of another 20-day fast that he has just completed, which is his second long fast this year. Recently there was an urgent call sent out by Brother Hawley throughout the Union of South Africa for a time of fasting and prayer, to which approximately 60,000 people responded.

God bless you in the work you are doing. You have indeed been the instrument in God's hands to awaken many thousands in many countries to this wonderful truth, that is so clear in the Word of God and yet so neglected.

With every kindest wish in the Lord,
Brother Len J. Jones, 197 President Ave.,
Kogarah, Sydney, N.S.W., Australia.

UNITED STATES

*"We believe that there is a great truth in prayer and fasting, since Jesus, when speaking of the devil in the lunatic child, whom the disciples could not heal, declared, 'This kind cometh not out but by prayer and fasting.' We do realize that fasting to be seen of men for self-aggrandizement is futile and profitless. But fasting with prayer has a place, as the Scriptures plainly teach. We know of no writer whom God has so signally used to bring out Scriptural truth on fasting, as Evangelist Franklin Hall. *We feel that 'Atomic Power with God' is the book of the hour for believers.* We trust that this book will be a special help to those whose prayers, for one reason or another, have not been answered.

"Many of the associates of 'The Voice of Healing' magazine, like myself, feel that fasting and prayer should have an important place in a successful salvation-healing ministry."

Brother Gordon Lindsay
Box 4097, Shreveport, La.

FASTED 40 DAYS AND RECEIVED GIFTS TO HEAL

Dear Brother in the Lord:

I am so happy for the Lord Jesus' truth of fasting and prayer.

After entering and completing a forty-day fast on March 30, God has helped in many miraculous ways. Since then Jesus has healed a regular landslide of CANCERS. One had cancer of the brain, and two had brain tumors. The work of Satan goes out quickly when prayer is made for these sick folk. The Lord is healing every kind of

---

*In recent months Brother Gordon Lindsay has been used with remarkable success in CITY-COMMUNITY-WIDE EVANGELISTIC HEALING CAMPAIGNS in auditoriums and tent cathedrals all over the country. His splendid, undenominational paper, "THE VOICE OF HEALING," can be had 10 months $1.00. Box 4097, Shreveport, La.

disease imaginable after the fast. I surely do recommend fasting to every minister who wishes to have a more successful healing ministry.

After just breaking another short fast of seven days, the Lord's power is all around the place where our prayer band meets.

I am director of "GOD'S WORLD PRAYER BAND" having approximately two thousand members. I would like very much to get your tracts on fasting and prayer into their hands. Will you please send me a quantity?

(Editor's note: It is prayer-fasting groups like these that are doing more than eye can see to bring a world revival.)

Sister May Eversole sends in a report of more fastings

Dear Brother Hall:

O, yes, I put into practice my faith in God. We are on a short fast now. I believe in it. Jesus did not show us how to do something that will kill us. I get very much out of fasting.

You are doing a nice work and it is helping to bring a world-wide revival of healings, and signs, and demonstrations of God's Spirit.

Thanks for the tracts. I have such a wonderful testimony. One time after finishing a twenty-eight-day fast, the Lord performed a miracle. I had a lot of bills to meet, and no money to pay them. *The God that multiplied the loaves and fishes, multiplied real money in my pocket-book. I opened it and there was over $200.00 in it.* I could pay my bills. Our prayer band is travailing, fasting and praying for a world revival.

Humbly, your Sister in Christ,
Sister May Eversole,
Director of "God's World Prayer Band"
1705 So. Cheyenne
Tulsa 14, Oklahoma.

CANADA—NEWFOUNDLAND

"It is with great interest and a very special delight that I give my whole-hearted recommendation to this completely NEW and DIFFERENT BOOK on the most important yet MOST NEGLECTED SUBJECT IN THE WHOLE REALM OF CHRISTIAN LIVING, 'FASTING AND PRAYER.'

Certainly, our author has had a very definite calling of God and unusual insight into the greatest desire of every earnest Christian—obtaining answers to prayer, and 'POWER WITH GOD.'

After reading the 'first sheets' before publication, IT HAS, in my own experience, BEEN WORTH MORE THAN ITS WEIGHT IN GOLD, and I'm positive that every earnest reader will acquire new and priceless knowledge and the most valuable information on how to secure a position with God SO THAT FAITH WILL 'MOVE THE MOUNTAINS' in your life.

The blessed contents of this book are by far the most complete and easily understood of all knowledge upon this subject that I have read in all other books combined.

I count it a privilege indeed to have found such 'inspired treasures' that give the true light on 'FASTING AND PRAYER.' THE SPIRITUAL VITAMINS' in this MASTERPIECE will bring forth 'SPIRITUAL GIANTS' and overcomers for God, and 'The Latter Rain will soon be here, as at Pentecost.' "

One year later: After having fasted forty days, and my wife, Barbara, twenty-one days, we have a far greater ministry in the Lord. Especially is this true concerning divine healing.

We have seen auditoriums packed out in Canada and Newfoundland. Hundreds were converted and healed from all kinds of diseases. Many had fasted previous to these great meetings—for days and weeks at a time. We feel that a world-wide move is on.

Your Servant in Christ,
Evangelist Dale Edward Hanson
Box 795, Tacoma, Wash.

5

TABLE OF CONTENTS

Chapters

Charts

Note: All Charts Designed and Drawn by Franklin Hall
Copyright 1946, 1950, and 1952
Printed in U.S.A.

★

DEDICATED
TO THE ONE WHO BLAZED THE TRAIL
THE
LORD JESUS CHRIST
THE EXAMPLE FOR US TO FOLLOW
HE WHO LEFT US THE KEY THAT UNLOCKS A GOLD MINE
FILLED WITH RICH TREASURES OF MANY
PRECIOUS EXPERIENCES
Mark 9:29

Chapter I

ATOMIC POWER WITH GOD

Fear and hatred stalk the world today. No one knows to what use men will put the newly discovered force of atomic energy. Many other devices of power would bring to pass the signs preceding the second coming of Christ as foretold in Luke 21:26: "Men's hearts failing them for fear, for the powers of heaven shall be shaken." And the cause of it all is the sad fact that man's spiritual development has lagged far behind his scientific development, with his many inventions and discoveries of the physical forces of nature.

Spiritually and emotionally, mankind on the whole is not far removed from the jungles, and therefore, incapable of handling the forces of nature that science has unleashed. Physical power, sufficient to disintegrate the entire world, is at the fingertips of a few, but there has been almost no development of spiritual power to control it. We have been wandering in the wilderness.

This spiritual power is actually within the reach of all followers of Christ. It is not so much that it has been forgotten, but rather that it has never been taught and learned. "The message of the Gospel is the power of God unto Salvation." Rom. 1:16. But we have overlooked a certain fundamental part of the Gospel message.

The writer shall endeavor to present a spiritual atomic power far greater than the physical force of all the atoms in the universe. Jesus Christ has made this power available to all His people, who will follow His Gospel pattern.

In 1848 A.D. the Aquarian Age was introduced to the world. The era of invention began and the machine came into being, along with the age of SPEED. Space and time began to shrink with the modern automobile, steam engine, and airplane. Distance ceased to be a barrier. More progress in scientific achievement was made in two generations than had been accomplished in the preceding two thousand years.

What about spiritual power? Except for a sprinkling here and there of the power of the Holy Spirit, scientific achievement has far out-distanced man's gains in things of the Spirit.

In the natural we have the automobile to speed us on our way. We have the steam engine shortening distance and also the airplane making distance no longer a barrier, etc. Radar and television bring distant objects nearer.

Surely if man's scientific achievement has increased in momentum, there must also be something to be found somewhere in the Word of God that will accelerate his SPIRITUAL PROGRESS. Like most scriptural truths, there is something; but only the wise shall understand it. The seemingly insignificance and misunderstanding may have been cause for its neglect. This latent power is FASTING AND PRAYER. This is a prayer that is prayed under the influence of fasting. Our spiritual progress will be like supersonic speed.

POWER THERMOMETER

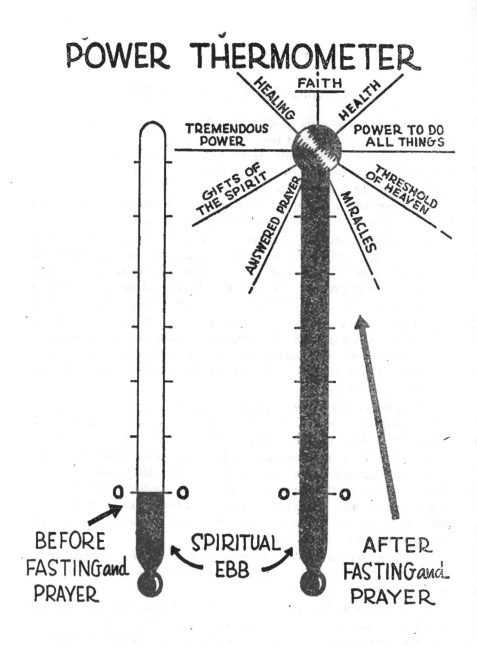

CHART No. 1. THE POWER THERMOMETER

The left side of the Chart reveals the average state of affairs before fasting. The right side shows the spiritual glories of a life filled to overflowing with the Holy Spirit. A long fast brings faith that works miracles, that brings healing for sickness and divine health for our mortal body, and a spiritual vision of the glory of heaven. Prayers of unbelief are converted into faith.

Thank God there is something which makes for Spiritual progress that is more scientific than anything man has accomplished to date, and which accomplishes wonders for our Spiritual welfare in a very short time. Without this knowledge, this goal might not be attained for many years, or perhaps NEVER. That something is FASTING AND PRAYER.

Our ultimate aim and desire should be the EXALTING OF JESUS CHRIST and the GLORIFYING OF HIM. Without prayer and fasting every Christian will more or less mark time and fail in their purpose. The most successful and the quickest method is through PRAYER AND FASTING; this pleases Jesus and in pleasing HIM we are availing ourselves of GREAT OPPORTUNITIES. "Delight thyself in the Lord; and He shall give thee the desires of thine heart." Ps. 37:4.

FASTING AND PRAYER make it far easier to DELIGHT OURSELVES IN THE LORD, it will give us the light ON THIS POWER. SPACE AND TIME TO GOD WILL SHRINK AND DISTANCE WILL CEASE TO BE, when one receives the potential light and puts it into practice.

If, as many believe, the unleashing of atomic energy is the prelude to the end of the earth, and if the seal judgments, the trumpet judgments, and the vial judgments of Revelation will soon be upon us, then the few who know and experience the saving power of God will do well to protect themselves against the day of His wrath, by a last great awakening through fasting and prayer. It will be the beginning of a new age for good, if the power of the Spirit is developed to a high degree by many through the use of the most powerful agent known to man, *fasting and prayer*. Without fasting, prayer becomes ineffectual. Fasting restores and amplifies prayer power.

A twenty-one, or forty-day prayer and fast will most assuredly hasten the Christian to such a deep and wonderful experience with God that twenty-one days will equal twenty-one years. Forty days will equal forty years. Experience shows that the forty-day period brings far greater results than a shorter time. It will bring one closer to God more quickly than any other way known.

Like the doctrine of divine healing, the doctrine of the Holy Spirit, etc., the truth of fasting has been sadly neglected. Many other forgotten Bible truths have been temporarily lost, only to be revived again in these "latter days" of this dispensation, the transition period between this and the millennial dispensation. The truth of fasting is being *revealed to us now that we may secure the greater things of God, that we may receive the "Gifts of the Spirit,"* and that a mighty world-wide revival of spiritual power will sweep over the world, with major signs and miracles in these last days. Fasting is the most potent power of the universe, and is placed at the disposal of every believer. A transformation in the body of Christ will begin, as Christians fast and pray.

The practice of fasting is as old as humanity. More than two thousand years ago, fasting was a custom advocated by the school of the natural philosopher, Asclepiades, for curative purposes. The Roman historian, Plutarch, said, "Instead of using medicine, fast a day." Traces of ancient fasting are to be found in ancient Chinese and Hindu writings, The Indians also practiced it.

It was used for religious purposes, as well as a method of restoring health. In the olden days they recognized the value of a fast, but today people look on fasting as a certain way to the grave. When a person speaks of fasting ten days, twenty-one days or more, many think it something horrible. It is through a lack of definite knowledge on the part of many, that this subject is so much misunderstood.

Fasting is a CORNERSTONE of the Christian religion, yet there is seldom, if ever, a complete sermon on the subject. Moreover, it is an important, basic truth of the Bible; yet we so often overlook its value.

So important is fasting in the Mohammedan religion, that they claim it to be *one of the four pillars* of the Mohammedan faith. This explains one of the reasons why there is more fervor and zeal in their religion, than in the Catholic or Protestant religions. Many Mohammedans take a thirty-day fast every year. Fervor and zeal are definitely a result of the fast. This is sadly lacking in our church of today. Fasting is mentioned in the Scriptures approximately one-third as much as prayer, yet our present day church member places it insignificantly in the background.

MOHAMMEDANS FAST 30 DAYS — FULL OF FANATICAL ZEAL

If Christians realized what great power and blessings they are missing, they would be only too eager and happy to fast. One of the reasons Satan cheats them out of this glorious experience, is through the misunderstanding and confusion that is so generally prevalent in regard to fasting.

Here is a testimony of a certain man who fasted fourteen days in one of my meetings. This was in 1945, when the world-wide fasting crusade was first launched.

UNDERWEIGHT—GAINS 29 POUNDS AFTER FASTING

"On the thirty-first day of December, 1945, after hearing Rev. Franklin Hall give some enlightening teaching on fasting, I started a consecration fast. I partook of no food during the entire fast of fourteen days. Water was taken for the purpose of cleaning out the system. I was a heavy smoker, and it seemed impossible to give it up, but on the third day of the fast *I had no further desire for smoking.* On the fourth day of the fast, *hunger left me entirely.* A little later *all weakness left;* and to my surprise I began feeling better and *stronger day by day.* I could *pray more earnestly,* and with greater results. Several days later, I *received the glorious baptism of the Holy Ghost.* I kept busy with my work which was not heavy. The fasting did not bother me much. What Brother Hall tells you about fasting is true, in our new spiritual consciousness our eyes are opened to discern the true nature of our former natural environment. And it worked out just that way in my life. It was a glorious experience.

FAST DELIVERS FROM SMOKING HABIT

"When I began the fast, I weighed one hundred and forty pounds. This was twenty-nine pounds underweight. At the conclusion of the fast, fourteen

THE BONDAGE OF UNBELIEF

No. II. Showing that DOUBT, UNBELIEF, and lack of FAITH prevent one from "taking off" and obtaining the greatest things that God has for those who will ONLY BELIEVE. MANY CHRISTIANS ARE NOT GETTING THEIR PRAYERS ANSWERED, ARE NOT BEING HEALED IN ANSWER TO PRAYER, AND ARE NOT SEEING THEIR LOVED ONES SAVED, JUST BECAUSE THEY FAIL TO HAVE "THE FAITH" THAT COMES BY PRAYER AND FASTING. Many pray, but how many follow JESUS' COMPLETE FORMULA, and FAST with their prayers, or go into THE FASTING prayer? Unbelief leaves and faith power is the product.

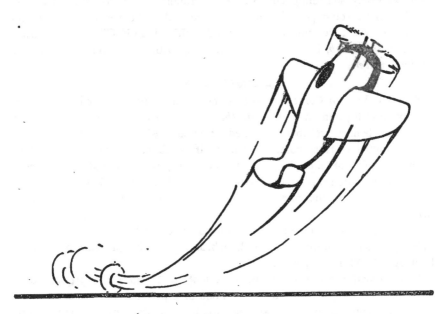

FAST AND TAKE OFF

No. III. Shows what will happen when the doubts and unbelief disappear through THE CONSECRATION FAST. The Christian gets "HIS SPIRITUAL WINGS." HIS UNANSWERED PRAYERS BECOME ANSWERED. DIVINE HEALING BECOMES AN ACCOMPLISHED FACT. JESUS IS EXALTED. The fasting Christian becomes a conductor of spiritual and supernatural power. He is enabled to carry on the works of a believer.

11

GAINS 29 POUNDS TO
NORMAL WEIGHT

days later, I had lost sixteen pounds, for I weighed a hundred and twenty-four pounds. Sixty days later *I had not only regained the lost weight, but also gained twenty-nine pounds more*, which was exactly what a man of my age should weigh, to the pound, that is, one hundred and sixty-nine pounds.

"Everyone told me that I looked better than they had ever seen me look, and I do *feel better than I have felt for twenty years*. All of my nervousness is gone, and I have better complexion, and best of all, I have received the

RECEIVES THE
HOLY SPIRIT

Holy Ghost, and have a much deeper experience with the Lord.

"My fast was shorter than many of the other brothers and sisters, but some day I hope to take a forty-day fast, as it certainly was a glorious experience to fast fourteen days. People do not know what they are missing."

Charles Wilson
4010 Euclid Avenue, San Diego 5, California.

When we speak of "ATOMIC POWER WITH GOD" we are using a term expressing something GREAT, and "Atomic Power" is as good an expression as we could possibly find to fill the bill. We are not exaggerating in the least when we compare "FASTING AND PRAYING" with the power of the *atomic bomb*, because, to the Christian, fasting will truly bring *atomic spiritual power*.

ATOMIC BOMB

Robert deVore in Collier's, quotes some of the figures released by the mission of investigation in Japan, on *the atomic bomb*. (The Nagasaki and Hiroshima bombs probably detonated at about 1800 feet altitude.)

"At 2,500 feet from point of impact—if bomb had reached earth—NOT from the point of explosion, 1,800 feet above, which would be farther— the pressure exerted was approximately SIX TONS TO THE SQUARE FOOT.

"At 4,200 feet, the pressure was a little more than ONE TON PER SQUARE FOOT.

"The first pressure noted above, is equivalent to a gale force of wind at 150 miles per hour, multiplied by 133, which equals the pressure of a wind blowing 20,000 miles per hour.

"The second pressure noted, is equivalent to 24 times the pressure of a 150-mile gale. Equals pressure of a 3,600-mile-per-hour hurricane.

"These enormous pressures are not wholly instantaneous, but are slightly delayed in their application, giving the water time to partially yield, and hence build up enormous wave effects. A vast, cone-shaped vortex is created, with a terrific "out-thrust," and subsequent return, of the displaced waters. No one can possibly calculate the true extent of this effect, but some physicists have stated that a wave of great height will be created.

"Consider the effect on water of the temperatures developed. The temperature of the atomic 'SUN' is estimated at FOUR MILLION DEGREES

Fahrenheit. Combustible materials of all kinds will burn at 1.4 miles distance. The ground temperature below the burst (at 1,800 feet altitude) was certainly more than 1,500 degrees Centigrade. WATER WAS INSTANTLY VAPORIZED," says DeVore. "Forests were scorched at 8,000 feet distance. All these facts point to the instantaneous vaporization of MILLIONS OF TONS OF WATER, to be thrown far into the upper atmosphere, and thence precipitated in torrential rains in distant parts of the world."

"This isn't a bomb at all," says General Farrell.

"These are the Fires of the Universe," says physicist Walter Graham.

This is the GREAT NATURAL POWER that man has discovered.

But greater still, and more potent, is the *spiritual atomic power with God,* that lies available to every Christian. The scientist can now use and harness the power of the material atom, but the Christian can use and harness the dynamic power of the great Creator of the atom. As the Creator is greater than that which He has created, so is the power wielded by the Christian, through fasting and prayer, greater than that wielded by the atomic scientist. It is the purpose of this volume to show the Christian a sure method, whereby he may obtain this mighty power, and may be able to move the omnipotent hand of God. This will be our spiritual, atomic jet-propulsion power.

Chapter II
WHAT IS FASTING?

Let us see what the word *fast* means. I believe misunderstanding here, causes much of our trouble about the subject of fasting. It is here that Satan deceives the average Christian.

Webster's, and also the Bible Dictionary, define fasting as, "abstinence from food. Especially as a religious observance." (FAST: "To abstain from food."). Now what does Webster say about water, as a food; or we may ask the question, "Is water food?"

First, we will consider Webster's definition of food, and it reads as follows: "Food: nutriment; nourishment in solid form."

Food and water-drinking are two different things. To do without water results in thirsting, and thirsting means, "a great desire to drink." Fasting will be understood better if we recognize these facts. One should not associate abstinence from water, with the subject of fasting; thus, we see the contradistinction between food and water.

The confusion that exists in the mind of the Christian who believes that he is not to drink water in a fast, MUST be overcome. This has prevented many people from fasting over a period of several days. Therefore they have been deprived of some of the very greatest blessings.

We will describe the protracted fast, or a "Complete Fast." We are dealing with the type of fast taken by the Lord Jesus Christ. A fast like that of

Paul, or Daniel: "Bible Fast." A complete fast is a fast from the time hunger leaves, until the time hunger returns. Such a fast may continue from twenty-one to forty days, depending on the individual, and also on the amount of time it takes you to get your prayers through to Heaven.

Fasting and Starvation are also two entirely different things.

DRINK WATER WHEN FASTING

To take a fast of this particular type, one must of necessity drink water. It is absurd for people to think about fasting and prayer without drinking water. Those who do this, do it in ignorance, and should be corrected by some constructive teaching. However, one may attempt a fast of a few days without drinking water, and find these facts to be immaterial.

Your body is the temple of the Holy Spirit, and to attempt a major fast without water, would defile and pollute the body. Scripture states: "If any man defile the temple of God, him shall God destroy." I Cor. 3:17.

Instructions are given by Christ in the Sermon on the Mount (Matt. 6:16-18) that "when thou fastest, anoint thine head, and *wash thy face; that* thou appear not unto men to fast, but unto thy Father, which is in secret, and thy Father which seeth in secret, *shall reward thee openly."* Washing the face is a sign of cleanliness. If it is good to wash your face to keep the toxic stains from face and body (washing being a type of cleanliness before God), then how much more logical it is to put water in your mouth, to clean out the corruption in the stomach. The stomach becomes deflated, collapsed, and depressed, when water is withheld long enough, and a person gets into bad shape. Without water, when fasting, the system will choke up, and *the body becomes filthy,* internally. The tongue, which is the upper part of the stomach, becomes heavily coated when fasting, showing visibly a part of the pollution that is in the stomach. Some doctors maintain that some food particles remain in the intestinal tract for more than a month, until putrefaction is worse than any garbage pail.

For the first few days of the fast, the stomach, tongue, and body, become heavily laden with the corruption that is trying to loosen itself. These particles that have remained in the stomach unassimilated, with other fecal matter, *require a great deal of water to break them down and help soften this material so that it can be eliminated.* Cramps, displeasure, misery, and other discomforts, are frequently experienced during this initial period. Water aids in the loosening and softening of this fecal matter without which the corruption will harden; the worms and bugs, which are nearly always present to some extent, will dry up on the intestines, the tongue will eventually thicken, and if the thirsting fast is prolonged, the individual will die, unless the Lord intervenes.

Paul knew the difference between "thirsting" and "fasting." He distinguishes them in II Cor. 11:27, "in hunger and thirst, IN

APOSTLE PAUL FASTED OFTEN FASTINGS OFTEN." If "hunger and thirst" were the same thing as "fasting," he would not have repeated the

14

same thing, any more than "cold" and "nakedness" are the same. Please note that a comma is inserted between each phrase. Paul was also educated.

A person should not only recognize the value of the fast, but whether your fast continues ten days, two weeks, forty days, or longer, your bowels should move every few days. If a person does not drink water while the fast is in progress, how can these channels of elimination function properly? The drinking of water will continue the process of cleaning while the fast continues. If the bowels do not move, please do not worry; there is no cause for alarm. Some folks' bowels do not move at all during the entire fast.

The drinking of water does not prevent one from drawing closer to God. Water is pure, and is a type of Salvation, and of the Holy Spirit. (John 4:14.) Water, unlike corruptible food, evaporates into the atmosphere, while food goes back to the earth. Water is not stimulating, while food is. Food feeds the appetites of carnality; water does not.

When an individual fasts, his pores becomes laden with toxins, especially his hands and face, therefore, he should bathe externally as often as possible.

In about two weeks, more or less, the average individual will have most of the wastes, poisons, toxins, fecal materials, etc., eliminated. That is, unless this individual has a deep-seated functional ailment. Even if this be the case, this should be relieved and healed if the fast is continued.

It is quite evident that Jesus took water while fasting forty days. There are four things that bear evidence in this regard. Shall we study our Lord's fast?

1. Matthew 4:2-11: "When he had fasted." We pointed that the *definition of fasting* does not exclude water drinking, and it does not mention that Jesus thirsted forty days, in the Scriptures. It is called a fast, and not a thirst.

2. "He was afterward an hungered." It does not say that He afterward thirsted. When a person does without both food and drink, water means far more to him than food. A man can go days without food, but this same individual can go but a very short time without water. Especially is this true in a hot and torrid climate.

   It seems very evident that Jesus did drink water. For at the time of the feeding the 4,000 (Mark 8:3), bread and fishes were offered after they had been fasting for three days, and Jesus, according to Scripture, did not offer them water, because they had no need of it. Water was available in the springs and brooks nearby.

3. Satan knew that He wasn't thirsty, because he did not tempt Him with water. He said, "Command that these stones be made bread."

4. The answer that the Son of God gave to Satan, is very evident. "Man shall not live by bread alone, but by every word that proceedeth out of the mouth of God." This seems to prove that He had partaken of water, for we must notice, in this connection, the failure to mention water.

You may ask if the fast that Jesus took was a supernatural one. No, this fast was not in any way a supernatural fast, for fasting is not supernatural, whether it is done by our Lord, or by the ones for whose salvation He paid the great price. "FASTING IS A SCIENCE." Anyone can fast for long periods of time, but only the Christian can expect supernatural results. The fast of Jesus can be said to be natural, on the ground that after His fast, He hungered. The natural hunger that had left his body for a time, returned again. This is true in any fast, if the fast is prolonged to its normal completion, when true hunger returns.

Critics who say that only Jesus could fast forty days, and that no one else can do so, are condemning something they know nothing about. They are in need of trying a fast themselves, then they would realize with a great awakening, the value of fasting.

The argument is brought to us that Moses fasted forty days. Please tell me what Scripture states this? In Exodus 34:28-29, we read, "And *he was there with the Lord forty days and forty nights;* he did neither eat bread, nor drink water." This abstinence was not called FASTING HERE, as failing to drink water is outside the meaning of the word. Why change the meaning of the word FASTING? On the mount, Moses was "there with the Lord for forty days"—this explains why Moses did not drink water—he was with the Lord, literally with the Lord. I am certain that if we were allowed to stand in His presence and be with God, we would neither have to eat, drink, or breathe, whether we were with Him forty days, or forty years. Actually the Lord Himself is our Food, Drink and Sustainer. This was true with Moses, because (Vs. 29)—"The skin of his face shone while he talked with Him." - The children of Israel were actually afraid of Moses. For he had received supernatural radiation that was far more real than food and drink. He had to veil his face to talk to them. When Moses died, he had the strength and constitution of a young man: "His eye was not dim, nor his natural force abated." Deut. 34:7.

ALLIGATORS
FAST SIX MONTHS

The world's largest alligator farm is in Los Angeles. Almost 2000 alligators are in captivity. Upon a recent visit, I learned that the creatures enter into a suspended animation for six months out of every year. They do not eat, drink or even breathe for six months out of the year. When it gets warm, they come out of their "anti-world" environment and gradually break into eating again. They have learned the art of eating, drinking and breathing that is incomparable to anything we humans can do. This suspended animation may be comparable to Moses' forty-day food-abstension without both food and water.

If any person fasts without taking water, and he can do so if he wishes, I must say, "Amen." However, any person can take short fasts of several days only, without water, as well as food, and still receive spiritual benefits for their sacrifice. See Esther 4:16, "Fast ye for me, and neither eat nor drink three days."

Doing without food will give you that spiritual uplift and power, with or without water. This has been proven many times. This fact is true in the fast of a few days, but we are now dealing with the long fast, which will give one power to do mighty things, seemingly the impossible, the fast that will break down denominational barriers and restore the body of Christ to its place of power and into the unity of the faith.

Dr. Tanner, who fasted over forty days on three occasions, declared that in the second half of each of the three fasts, the unspeakable glories of the world beyond were revealed to him. Dr. Tanner lived to be ninety-two years of age, and gave credit to fasting for his longevity of life. In Dr. Tanners' day they ridiculed Christ's fast, saying, "nobody could fast that long." Dr. Tanner challenged them. His first fast lasted over forty days, and was under observation by his disbelievers. He was weighed and checked daily; thus he broke down the ridicule of fasting in his time. Dr. Tanner was a physician as well as a Christian. His first fast was so glorious,

BLACK HAIR REPLACES GREY HAIR AFTER 40-DAY FAST

that later on he took additional fasts of over forty days. After his last fast *a crop of new black hair appeared in place of the grey hair.*

Luther fasted for days at a time, while translating the Bible, and herein undoubtedly lies the secret of his unrivaled translation, and

MARTIN LUTHER FASTED

it is also responsible for bringing the reformation revival of his time. His great faith was likewise largely through the revelation of God's presence, which is revealed through PRAYER AND FASTING. Thank God for men that get a vision, who will go all out.

LUST HUNGER

"And they tempted God in their heart by asking meat for their lust. Yea, they spake against God; they said, Can God furnish a table in the wilderness?" God at first did not readily give them food as they did not actually need it. This food was wanted to satisfy an appetite of LUST which is habit hunger.

God did, however, give them "angel's food" and "sent them meat to the full. He gave them their own desire." And they were destroyed. "He gave them their request; but sent leanness into their soul." See Ps. 78:29-34.

A close study of the Scriptures will show clearly that sin is sin. The partaking of an over-amount of food is classed in the category of sin, because the same damage is done to the body, as by alcohol, tobacco, dope, etc. This fact is also emphasized by Jesus Christ when He was tempted by Satan for forty days. He was tempted to command the stones to become food. Jesus' answer was very effective, "MAN SHALL NOT LIVE BY BREAD ALONE, BUT BY EVERY WORD THAT PROCEEDETH OUT OF THE MOUTH OF GOD." See Deut. 8:3 and Matt. 4:4. Again Jesus shows what value the world will place on food when "The Son of Man cometh. For as in the days that were before the flood, they were EATING AND DRINKING. So shall also the coming of the Son of Man be." Jesus is not criticizing the eating to live. But He is greatly condemning the "living to eat," that is so prevalent everywhere. It is a sign of the last days. The sign that tells us that the coming of our Lord draweth nigh.

In Matt. 24:37, 38, and Luke 21:34, eating is placed ahead of drinking.

Chapter III

THE BACKGROUND FOR REVIVAL

"SANCTIFY A FAST, CALL A SOLEMN ASSEMBLY:" Joel 2:15.

To see our loved ones saved, souls converted and a sweeping revival come in our midst; to have God work miracles, and heal our diseases, and pour out His Holy Spirit, we must start a fast and prayer in the home. "LORD, let it begin in me!" Even if you are the only converted member of the family, you can get hold of God in such a way, by FASTING AND PRAYER that Jesus, seeing your fervor and zeal developing the faith for the salvation of your loved ones, will most certainly hear your prayer and convert them. Many times a person has done this, and not only were the loved ones converted, but the Lord so rewarded them that an "old-fashioned" revival swept the whole community, saving, healing, and blessing mightily with the Spirit.

In 1932 the Holy Spirit led the author into his first revival meeting. He knew only three families in the Oklahoma oil town, Nowata. One of these families believed and practiced *fasting and prayer*. Together we prayed and fasted ahead of time for the meeting that we knew God was going to give us. The foundation was properly laid for a revival, and a revival we certainly did have. There was no building big enough to take care of the crowd, so we secured three acres of ground and had an open air meeting (this was in July). People packed the place from the first service. We kept building seats, and the crowd continued to increase every evening. People gathered from all over Northeastern Oklahoma and Southeastern Kansas for the meetings. Scores of people were healed of all types of afflictions. One lady who had been in a car wreck with broken ribs, was carried to the services on pillows; she was instantly healed. A deaf and dumb boy was enabled to hear and speak. A man who could not lift his arm, and had been paralyzed, was healed of his paralysis and was able to lift his arm. Many more received notable healings. Folks were under the power of His Spirit. Many were baptized.

Within three months from the time we started the meeting, we built a church, and got it paid for, so that the people could **FASTING BUILDS A CHURCH AND PAYS OFF THE MORTGAGE** continue to have a place to worship in truth and in Spirit. ALL OF THESE RESULTS WERE TRACED DIRECTLY TO PRAYER AND FASTING. My brother assisted me in the meeting. The church is still progressing for the glory of God to this day.

FASTING FOR THE HOME

If church leaders and parents, the heads of churches and homes, do not live up to *"the faith which was once delivered unto the saints,"* how can we expect our children to be saved? FASTING WAS AS SURELY A PART

OF THE FAITH that was once delivered unto the saints as anything else. Fasting is one of the great foundation piers of the Christian religion. The structure of the Christian religion is built upon the vital truth of prayer and fasting. It was a vital part of the early church. Therefore, the great results that accompanied it were seen in those early days.

The lack of fasting explains the great "falling away," the "losing their first love," because man cares more for his "desire-nature," than for the fortification of his soul. People have failed to follow the complete pattern of the *faith formula* of Christ, given in Matthew, chapter seventeen, or Mark 9:29. They not only failed to have power to do the impossible, but after the days of the apostles the church became powerless, and eventually began to say that the days of healing were over; that the miracles were not for them anymore; the Holy Spirit, after the Bible pattern, was forsaken, and the power of the apostolic age was lost. Many splits soon divided the church of Jesus Christ. The men of old that had fasted and prayed, and who had power with God to perform miracles of healing, had either died, or had been martyred. The younger generations discontinued the use of fasting.

Matt. 9:15: "The days will come, when the Bridegroom shall be taken away from them, and then shall they fast. How many

"THEN SHALL THEY FAST" "Children of the Bridegroom" are obeying Christ's command, "then shall they fast"? It is here that our Lord lays upon us, as the children of the bridegroom the duty of fasting: *"When the Bridegroom shall be taken from them, then shall they fast."* And as long as our Bridegroom tarries, just so long should we continue to fast, until that happy day when He returns and fasting need be no more.

It wasn't as necessary to fast while Jesus was here on earth, because He had fasted to obtain the more perfect faith. After He left we could have had through FASTING the same power and FAITH that His visible presence gave.

INDIAN TRIBES PRACTICE FASTING

Many, if not all, the American Indian tribes sought revelation of the Great Spirit through Prayer and Fasting. When they had famines, food shortages, lack of rain, etc., the Great Spirit was sought through prayer and fasting, and their prayers were answered. In certain tribes nearly all Indian children who came to the age of puberty were set aside in prayer

CHILDREN FAST and a *fast of seven to ten days*, to burn out, so to speak, the evil sex desires, so that they would have high moral thoughts, and live a high spiritual life. As they grew and developed into manhood or womanhood the practice of fasting was continued. Is not this a lesson for the American home of today? If this method were taught and put into practice in our day, we would not see as many disobedient sons and daughters who are the source of such grief and heartaches to their parents.

A survey was recently disclosed by a writer of the well-known periodical, the "Presbyterian," which reveals facts that are alarming: Out of 49,000,000 young people in the United States, 36,000,000 have never set foot inside any church, of any creed. This same writer in another survey, learned from questionnaires sent to 55,000 children of school age, that 16,000 of them had never heard of the Ten Commandments, let alone quote the Lord's prayer.

FASTING FOR CHILDREN

Fasting is beneficial to children. When a child becomes ill, very often several meals, or several days fasting, will fix up everything. Many children as they grow and eat rich foods, develop a pimpled complexion. The source of the condition is in the stomach. The stomach tries to unload its poisonous material in the blood, and to some extent through the skin. Only a few days of fasting will eradicate all traces of the symptoms. If proper eating is undertaken, it should not return. Scores of minor and major ailments of young people could be whipped by a short fast. Girls would not find it necessary to wear "make-up," if they would fast and pray more. A natural, healthy complexion would be the result.

Babies quite frequently suffer from over-feeding rather than under-feeding. If one considers how small a baby is, and analyzes the great quantity of food that is given to him, in proportion to the food of an adult, one would find it enormous. Adults would have to drink twenty-one quarts of milk daily, to be the equivalent of a baby's food. The "colic," "gases in the stomach," "belching," "vomiting," "diarrhea,' and many other baby disturbances can be quickly eliminated by a fast of one or more meals.

METHODIST MINISTER GETS CHURCHES REVIVED

Dear Brother Hall:

I am a Methodist minister who received your book two years ago.

After fasting and praying ten days for a revival in three Methodist churches that I am in charge of, God stirred and sent revivals in our midst. The Lord richly blessed us in many ways. A Roman Catholic and his Protestant wife were among those gloriously saved.

In one of my churches an Italian lady to whom I gave one of your books, went on a fast of twenty-three days for her old Catholic mother who came from the old country, was blind, and about to die. She was praying to beads and images. She became interested in Jesus and learned how to pray to the Lord. Finally she was gloriously saved.

The lady who fasted twenty-three days was hopelessly afflicted with kidney stones. The doctor could do nothing for her, and said an operation would be necessary. Well praise the Lord, she has not had an attack since her fast two years ago.

Before I became acquainted with fasting, my people said, "We have never heard of fasting." I said, "Bless your heart, have you never read your Bible?"

Pray for me as I work in these Methodist churches, and kindly send a good supply of pamphlets on fasting.

Yours in Him,
R. B. Krape, Woodbine,
R.F.D. No. 1, Eldora, N. J.

We urge you to obtain the author's book, *"Glorified Fasting,"* This is volume two of the set of five different books. "Glorified Fasting" gives the "whys," "whats," "whens," and "wherefores" of Fasting. It goes completely into this subject in a different manner and approaches it from a different viewpoint. Our complete library set of five different books on FAITH, will be sent to you postpaid for $5.00. These volumes give faith treatments.

Chapter IV

JESUS' FAST

Three of the most highly developed spiritual giants of the Bible are three who fasted for the full length of FORTY DAYS. First and foremost is our Lord Jesus Christ who "was led up of the Spirit into the wilderness, and when He had fasted forty days and forty nights . . ." Second, we have the mightiest spiritual giant of the entire Old Testament, Moses, who "was there with the Lord forty days and forty nights; he did neither eat bread, nor drink water," and who, on a second occasion, "fell down before the Lord forty days and forty nights; I did neither eat bread, nor drink water." And third, we have the mighty prophet Elijah, that called down the "fire of the Lord that consumed the burnt sacrifice," and "who prayed earnestly that it might not rain, and it rained not on the earth by the space of three years and six months," and we read of him that he went without eating, "in the strength of that meat forty days and forty nights unto Horeb the mount of God." When the apostle James wanted to select a man who was an example of "effectual fervent prayer," he chooses Elijah, a man who could go for forty days without eating. It is the man who fasts, who has the spiritual character that can pray through on a really big job. When God said that He would destroy the whole Israelite nation for their sin, it is "Moses His chosen," who fasted forty days, and "stood before Him in the breach, to turn away His wrath, lest He should destroy them." Psalm 106:23.

Other folk of great importance and high spirituality that fasted during long periods when they were under great mental strain and tribulation, are Anna the prophetess, David, Daniel, John the Baptist, and Paul. A close study of their lives shows they gained great spiritual strength by fasting and prayer, that otherwise they would not have received.

Fasting was part and parcel of the very life of Christ, and yet this very essential part of Christian life has been ignored by many Christians as if it were an unsolved mystery. It was never meant to be hidden, and should never have been so overlooked. This may explain why we have not had a more complete outpouring of the latter rain. Surely such a stupendous truth cannot continue to be a secret hidden in plain sight for over nineteen hundred years. The strides and progress of man in other channels have been so enlightening and progressive. Surely we feel that it is time, long past due, for all to "labour for Christ," in whom are hidden all treasures of wisdom and knowledge. Try this truth that gives such a treasure-house of riches and strength. We do not fast to merit favor from God or as a penance.

We read that "Jesus was led up of the Spirit into the wilderness to be tempted of the devil." And the very next sentence tells us that He fasted.

FASTING ASSURES VICTORY OVER TEMPTATION

Why did He fast at the very time He was being tempted? For we read in Luke's Gospel that He was "forty days tempted," and in those same forty days "He did eat nothing." What is the connection between *temptation* and *fasting?* Is it not that fasting is the mightiest possible preparation of soul, to insure victory over temptation? And would we not do well to follow our Lord's example, and avail ourselves of this mighty weapon with which to meet and overcome him "who goeth about as a roaring lion, seeking whom he may devour"?

We are not told in Matthew, chapter four, the reason for His fast. But in Matthew, chapter seventeen, Jesus explains it. Before this time His disciples were not able to bear this teaching. The great revelation of why He fasted, was shown when He healed this lunatic boy, and answered the question that the disciples had asked Him: "Why could not we cast him out?" Matt. 17:19.

Please remember that Christ, as well as being God, was also in the flesh as man.

It seemed that the disciples had become a reproach, or disgrace to Christ, because they could not heal this individual. They apparently were ashamed of themselves so they came to Jesus secretly, to ask of Him the reason why they were not able to cast out the demons. Then the secret of Jesus' fast was revealed, and He showed to them and to us what *"Super-Atomic Power"* one can have. Anyone can have that power, thank the Lord. All can have it who will follow the instructions given by Him, and plainly taught throughout the Bible. *"Have Faith* as a grain of mustard seed . . . and nothing shall be impossible unto you . . . by prayer and fasting." Matt. 17:20, 21.

The disciples were helpless. No one could give help in this major prayer problem except One. That Person had fasted forty days and forty nights, and He was the only one in the midst who had so fasted. Praise His name!

However, Jesus clearly shows that anyone who had had a prayer and fasting experience, could cast out the evil spirit, for He says, "This kind cometh out by prayer and fasting." Our Lord teaches here the big difference, between prayer alone, and *prayer, combined with fasting.*

In that momentous struggle of forty days of fasting JESUS had AVAILED HIMSELF OF THE MOST POWERFUL AID AT HIS DISPOSAL. Jesus fasted in order to secure His perfect faith from His humanity side, and He urged fasting upon His disciples to remedy their weak faith. He declared that *they would fast,* using the words, "Then will they fast," and gave directions in Matthew chapter six, which are intended to insure to all of His followers the same benefits of fasting which He obtained. The disuse of fasting is in direct opposition to the practice, example, and the teaching, of Christ.

There is no record of Christ healing the sick, or performing any miracle, until after he had fasted forty days and forty nights. After this mighty fast, and not before, He was fully equipped, capable, and prepared for any and all emergencies. *At this moment, how much Faith have you at your disposal, to meet any obstacle?*

When Jesus was twenty-one years old the record shows He had not yet performed a miracle. At twenty-five, he still had no healings, miracles, and no manifestation of His Divine Sonship. He became twenty-six, twenty-seven, twenty-eight and twenty-nine years of age, and yet, no miracles or manifestations. Why? He had not received the fullness of the Holy Spirit, and had not spent forty days fasting. It was necessary for Jesus to be prepared and have all the spiritual equipment, before He went forth to perform His mighty works.

Satan's rage knew no bounds at the conclusion of Christ's fast, and he sought ways and means to subdue Him. Christ could not have been tempted by something He did not need. But we read that "when He had fasted forty days and forty nights, He was afterward an hungered." Now, Jesus could turn these stones into bread and yield to an appetite similar to the one Eve yielded to in the Garden of Eden. The answer that Jesus gave was not only an answer to Satan, but throws a challenge to all humanity: "Man shall not live by bread alone, but by every word that proceedeth out of the mouth of God." Matt. 4:4.

Jesus received the Holy Spirit, but this did not seem sufficient. It requires fasting and prayer to operate the Holy Ghost.

Jesus, at thirty years of age, only after praying and fasting forty days and forty nights, began to manifest Himself as the Son of God with all power, signs, and wonders. There was such an awakening! Fasting is the most powerful means at the disposal of every child of God. Fasting literally becomes prayer to the praying Christian, prayer that is as different as an atomic bomb compared to an ordinary bomb. Prayer alone is like the ordinary bomb, and the fast with prayer, is comparable to the Super-Atomic Bomb.

Jesus knew the positive value of prayer and fasting, and was confident that they were the only means to the end that He sought. Jesus fasted in order that prayer might become prayer in the highest sense—might reach its highest intensity. He blazed the way that we are to follow. Although Jesus knew He was the Son of God, this assurance was stamped more indelibly upon Him by the prayer and fasting of forty days.

Satan was not too much interested in Christ until He was ready to MANI-FEST HIS SONSHIP. Then and only then, after His forty-day fast, was Satan right on the job, ready to assail Him in every way that he could. If Christ was immune, and could not have sinned or yielded to Satan at this time, then this would have been the greatest farce that the world has ever seen. Surely, Christ could have yielded to this temptation. Satan knew that He could, and set about to try Him. Jesus Christ, with fasting back of Him, was well prepared for the attack. We are so thankful that although Jesus was tempted and tried in every manner, as we are, yet He did not yield to temptation; He victoriously overcame Satan. We can likewise be an overcomer.

Fasting and praying, then, aids us in overcoming temptations and trials, and prepares us to meet the attacks of the enemy.

When we fast and pray, we should never lose sight of the fact that our FAST must be for THE GLORY OF GOD, that Jesus shall continually have ALL PRAISE, HONOR, AND GLORY. A continual PRAISE, along with our PRAYERS, SHOULD ALWAYS BE IN OUR HEARTS TO OBTAIN THE FULLEST SPIRITUAL RESULTS. In other words, make it a time of FASTING AND PRAISE FOR THE GLORY OF GOD. Jesus, our MEDIATOR, is the ONE WHO WILL SEE THAT WE ARE RICHLY REWARDED. THE ONE WHO "BOUGHT US WITH HIS OWN BLOOD" IS CERTAINLY WORTHY OF MUCH PRAISE AND HONOR. A PRAISE THAT CONTINUALLY FLOWS FROM THE HEART IS LIKE INCENSE THAT RISES TO THE THRONE OF GOD. The four beautiful LIVING CREATURES of Rev. 4:8, *"REST NOT DAY AND NIGHT,* SAYING, HOLY, HOLY, HOLY, LORD GOD ALMIGHTY, WHICH WAS, AND IS, AND IS TO COME."* This may sound very foolish to the sinner, but to the child of God it sounds like, "HALLELUJAH!" AMEN.

FASTS 40 DAYS—SEES MIGHTY DETROIT REVIVAL

At nineteen years of age I was dying with the flu. My temperature was 106 degrees! **DYING WITH FEVER** It was on this death bed that I surrendered completely to God. I promised the Lord I would preach the Gospel, if He would heal me. Then I was caught up to heaven for twelves hours, and saw the **CAUGHT UP TO HEAVEN** glories of that wondrous land. When I came back I was perfectly healed, ready to work for Him who raised me up so miraculously. Praise His name!

Even at that young age, God said, "If I would be faithful in fasting and praying, He would raise up workers all over the world in their own tongues." He also gave me Mark 10:29-30 as a call to travel and do exploits in His name. I was shown many other things as I started my life with fastings and praying like Paul. Many times my fastings were from three days to a week and longer. In some of my fasts the Lord gave me much revelation concerning the time we live. In the beginning of my Christian experience, while on a two-weeks' fast, I cried and prayed until Jesus became so real that one night He appeared in my room. The room was all lighted up, brighter than the sun! Jesus stood at the foot of my bed, and around Him was a light much brighter than the sun. This great experience was very impressive and for a long time I seemed to be walking on air. Shortly after that, while fasting five days, the Lord filled me with a peculiar experience. A missionary from Rome told me that I was speaking a message, and glorifying and praising the Lord in his Italian language. Yet I had never spoken Italian before. It must have been the Holy Spirit talking. The missionary interpreted what I was saying into English.

After giving up my job, I went on a partial fast for three months, eating only once a day. The Lord gave me intercession for souls.

After praying and fasting seven days to see sinners converted, and to ask the wonderful Lord to give me more of Him, the Lord sent a revival meeting to Dayton, Ohio, where the Lord healed a multitude of sick folk and converted many souls. My prayer was also answered in another way when a lady gave me Dr. Franklin Hall's book on **READS "ATOMIC POWER WITH GOD"** fasting and prayer. This deeper fasting experience was what I wanted. I was now able to fast longer than a week or two. I was so burdened for sinners, and that their bodies might be healed, that I could hardly sleep at night. With my longer fasting I could get greater victories for my intercession. I could see what God will do when multitudes begin to fast. Jesus showed me that before long there would be workers all over the world who would fast and travail for souls. This would bring great revivals, yes, greater than the world has ever seen, even greater than when Jesus was here.

It would seem unbelievable in the natural, if it were not for this Word: "The works that I do shall ye do also; and greater works than these shall ye do; because I go unto my Father." John 14:12.

After fasting forty days without food, with Jesus strengthening me, I saw many more miracles and demonstrations of the Holy Spirit. I saw the "dry bones" of Ezekiel take life. As I continued to agonize and weep for lost souls, the spirit of heaviness was upon me to such an extent that it seemed that my spirit would leave the body. I saw, in a vision, thirty thousand souls appear before me, finding Christ as their Saviour, in a coliseum in Detroit, Michigan. (SINCE THIS REVELATION TO BROTHER BARTH, THERE HAVE COME TO DETROIT SOME MIGHTY HEALING-SALVA-TION-OUTPOURINGS, through Sister Beal, Brother Wm. Branham, Brother T. Osborn, Brother G. Lindsay, Brother F. Bosworth and LITTLE DAVID.) I saw, in a vision, another 10,000 find Jesus in an open field. Many churches, auditoriums and big tents were packed. A mighty revival is coming through fasting and prayer, but I was shown how the wealthy Laodicean churches were dealt out judgment. Their false leaders were given the judgment of Ananias and Sapphira, when they lied to the Holy Spirit.

When I was reading Brother Hall's books on fasting, the sweetest incense came down from heaven, setting a seal of approval upon them. They present a teaching of Jesus Christ that, if followed, will truly bring a world revival among dying and lost humanity. I believe this is Jesus Christ's truth, and it is the message of the hour for cold, sleepy and backslidden Christians.

Your Brother in Christ,
Leonard Barth, 1776 Cherry St.
Youngstown 8, Ohio.

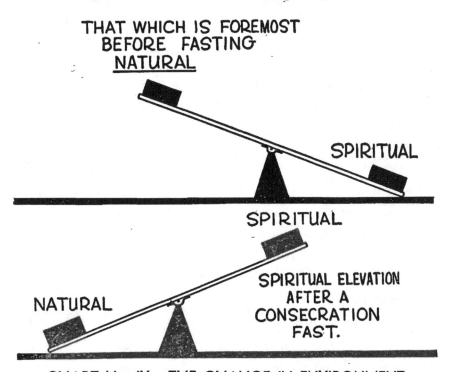

THAT WHICH IS FOREMOST
BEFORE FASTING
NATURAL

SPIRITUAL

SPIRITUAL

NATURAL

SPIRITUAL ELEVATION
AFTER A
CONSECRATION
FAST.

CHART No. IV. THE CHANGE IN ENVIRONMENT

Chart showing WHY ONE DOES NOT HAVE "FAITH AS A GRAIN OF MUSTARD SEED." THE CARNAL NATURE IS ELEVATED ABOVE THE SPIRITUAL. FASTING AND PRAYER LOOSEN THE NATURAL GRIP OF THE WORLD SO THAT THE POWER OF GOD AND FAITH MAY BE MORE MANIFESTED. We become conductors of spiritual power.

FASTING CAUSES CHANGE IN ENVIRONMENT

"And He humbled thee, *and suffered thee to hunger,* and fed thee with manna, which thou knewest not, neither did thy fathers know; that He might *make thee know that man doth not live by bread only,* but by every word that proceedeth out of the mouth of the Lord doth man live." Deut. 8:3. This depicts in a wonderful manner how God sought to change the environment of the children of Israel that they might be transformed from the habits and lusts of the old environment of the land of Egypt, and made ready for the new environment of the land of Canaan. Much spiritual preparation was needed before they would be prepared to enter the new land of promise. The bondage of Egyptian environment was rooted in their minds, bodies and souls. They still lusted after the old things of sin. their old habits, and the traditions of the world. Because they failed to accept the forced fast that was put upon them by an all-loving and wise Lord, they were required to break down this environment the hard, long way. By failing to fast and break down the bondage of environment in a few days time, and then march right into the promised land, they were consequently compelled to *march around in circles for forty years,* as many of us are doing today, that the flesh might be broken, and that the old stubborn, bound individuals might die, before taking the promised land.

We too can miraculously change our Christian environment in ten days or more of fasting. It would otherwise require many long years. It might be doubtful if much progress could be made, the long way.

ENVIRONMENT CHANGED—SPIRITUAL GIFTS RECEIVED

Dear Brother Hall:

I can never tell you in words what the teaching of fasting and prayer, as set forth in your book, "Atomic Power with God," has meant to me. I was earnestly seeking more on this subject, when this book fell into my hands. I simply devoured its great truth, backed by the Word of God. Immediately I went on a consecration fast; God came on the scene, and shortly I received gifts of healing.

I feel that you have the message of the hour, the one that will awaken the sleeping church, and cause men and women to become stirred to the realization that Jesus is coming soon. God is pouring out His gifts of the Spirit in these days. I attribute the success of my ministry to the message God gave you on fasting and prayer, that you so generously made many sacrifices to give to the body of Jesus Christ.

Your Sister in His service,
Evangelist Thelma Nickel, 405 S. Wheeling Ave., Tulsa 4, Oklahoma.

REVIVAL IN SOUTH AFRICA AFTER FASTING 40 DAYS

1150 Pretorius St., Pretoria, South Africa.

Dear Brother Hall:

Mrs. R. Retief gave me your books on fasting. After reading them I was convinced that your teaching was right. I started to fast on the 27th of May, and started to break the fast on 6th of July—thus having fasted forty days.

I had fasted before for a day or two and I thoroughly believe in it. I have been practicing the healing message too. The 40-day fast did not unduly inconvenience me. I became weak at the end, after losing 38 pounds. I sought glory for my Lord through **GETS MONEY TO PAY HIS DEBTS** consecration. The fullness of the Holy Spirit, and the conversion of the people who come to the place where I have oversight, was desired and received. Several families were converted and I received money to pay my debts. My eyes that were bothering me were improved . . .

Just after the fast I spoke to a Women's Association upon "REVIVAL" through fasting and prayer. Now several of the women are fasting two days a week for a revival in this country. A revival also came to our church.

Yours in Him, J. Keith Craig.

Chapter V

ONE HUNDRED REASONS WHY WE SHOULD FAST

"I do not need to fast. I am too thin." "You won't catch me starving myself to death." "I get too weak." "I am too lazy to fast." "It is ridiculous to think the Lord expects me to fast. I will never fast unless the Lord puts a fast on me." These and other remarks are made by folk who have practically no understanding at all as to what fasting is all about. Only narrow minded folk and fanatics condemn something they know nothing about. If you should be one who has never fasted ten continuous days in your lifetime, and never received light on the *power* and revival force of protracted fasting, why not be open-minded enough to search the Bible and its facts, to see for yourself, and not ignore such a major teaching of the Word of God? The practice of this message is now helping to bring a World Revival before Jesus comes.

In our earlier evangelistic tours, where we have had the privilege of contacting thousands of Christians from many different denominations, we had yet to find more than several folk in a city who had ever heard or read, one single complete sermon on the subject. Several years later, we find this condition changing.

Again, some are inclined to believe that fasting may have only one or two small virtues. Maybe it is beneficial, they think, to rid heavy folk of their fat, or that the suffering one goes through it like penance, and that the denial of food blesses the Lord through our sacrifices.

A number of reasons are given here, showing the importance of consecrated *fasting to Jesus:*

1. Fasting becomes prayer to the praying Christian. "I humbled my soul with fasting; and my prayer returned unto my bosom." Psalm 35:13.
2. Fasting developes humility.
3. Fasting removes pride.
4. Fasting intensifies the POWER OF PRAYER.
5. Fasting is a form of worship.
6. Fasting reaches and obtains what prayer alone cannot. Matt. 17:17-21.
7. Fasting REMOVES UNBELIEF, Matt. 17:20, 21.
8. Fasting is the greatest FAITH PRODUCER. Matt. 17:21.
9. Fasting is more closely related to FAITH, THAN ANY OTHER CHRISTIAN WORK.
10. Fasting is the very threshold of FAITH, but because it is not understood, it is frequently overlooked.
11. Fasting will "BLITZKRIEG" the devil.
12. Fasting is the speediest method known to spiritual success.
13. Fasting brings one face to face with reality.

14. Fasting brings one into direct contact with UNBELIEF, so that it can be removed. Unbelief can never be fully comprehended, until one fasts ten to forty days.

15. Fasting masters the old man, and gives him a powerful beating.

16. Fasting pleases the Spirit. "THE FLESH AND THE SPIRIT ARE CONTRARY THE ONE TO THE OTHER."

17. By thus mortifying the flesh, it brings the believer into not only favor with God, but also gives him fame and favor with mankind. Lk. 4:14.

18. Fasting will mortify one's members to break bondage. Col. 3:5.

19. Fasting prevents the flesh from going on a raid.

20. Fasting is the most spiritual process to bring a revival.

21. Fasting leaves the natural and takes one quickly into the spiritual realm.

22. Fasting will undo the sins of intemperance.

23. Fasting will break bad habits.

24. Fasting is self-chastisement, and will prevent many chastisements of the Lord from coming upon us.

25. Fasting, when properly entered into, is the surest method of consecration and sanctification.

26. Fasting is the easiest way for backsliders to come home. Study David's fasts. It is not a form of penance and will not buy favor. It is a process.

27. Fasting slows down carnality and un-natural desires.

28. Fasting places our natural appetites in a dormant condition, so that physical pleasures are not enjoyed. With pleasurable appetites static, God can come near us, and we near Him. He is contacted. A revival begins.

29. Fasting brings one nearer to Christ than any other known process.

30. Fasting will see our unanswered prayers answered. "Nothing shall be impossible unto him . . . by PRAYER AND FASTING." Matt. 17:21.

31. Fasting changes one's environment from the natural to the SPIRITUAL. A revival of power in the spirit begins to grow.

32. Fasting sees a life of defeat transformed into a life of VICTORY; thus giving HEALING and new life, to both the body and the soul.

33. Fasting develops the fruit of the Spirit and assists one in receiving spiritual gifts.

34. Fasting consumes and burns out the very roots of fleshly lusts.

35. Fasting brings one into the misery and suffering of the fleshly nature in such a manner that one can see himself in the same light that Jesus sees him. We see our unworthiness, but we see also that Jesus made unto us worthiness, on our behalf. We are now worthy through Christ.

36. Fasting gives the child of God spiritual manifestations.

37. Fasting will always give one the anointing of the Spirit for work.

38. Fasting always brings revelations and better understanding of the Bible. Sometimes visions and unspeakable glory will also be manifested.

39. Fasting enlarges our capacities. Many of us have only a thimble-size capacity. We might be full at times, but how full? Shouting and spiritual

emotion does not always indicate how large our capacities are. A person may be running over with only a thimble-size capacity. Fasting will give a bushel, and a well-size, capacity to enjoy the riches of heaven, glory and power. We then can receive rewards, depending on how long and how properly we fast and pray.

40. Spiritual efficiency is highly accelerated through the fast, so the individual, being a more efficient conductor of spiritual forces, likewise becomes a powerful conductor of the *healing power* of Christ, whether for his personal body, or for the needs of others. Vital spiritual forces pour through individuals who have been in fastings.

41. Spiritual forces flowing through fasting people cause them to become more receptive to the spiritual gifts that are being poured forth today.

42. Fasting places the candidate's sense faculties in such a position that they cannot war against faith. Faith springs forth more readily, and the vital contact is made for receiving divine healing or any other prayer objective from Jesus.

43. Our strongholds of the flesh are pulled down, so that faith has no real barriers. II Cor. 10:3-5. Fasting casts down reasonings, so that we will not listen to the evidence that our senses may bring forth, but we let faith loose.

44. Fasting will stay the hand of judgment.

45. Fasting being a spiritual process, we learn how to believe that God will do what He tells us He will do, and we begin doubting the flesh and the devil, rather than doubting God's Word any longer.

46. That which could not come about, without fasting and prayer, has now come to pass, because thousands of Christians are fasting longer than at any other time since the days of Christ. As the author has predicted many times, a revival was certain to come when men and women put this vital process into practice on a large scale. Today there is strong evidence to support the fact, that the mighty evangelistic healing campaigns the world over are the result of fasting and prayer and that thousands are receiving spiritual gifts as never before since the time of Christ. Not just a measly fast of a few meals, but major fasts are underway by many of the saints. These major fastings are from ten to forty or more days. Many who do not understand fasting or the potency of long fasts, may be skeptical.

47. Fasting is a powerful process and is similar to that of faith. Very few understand or even have much faith, although most folk desire to brag that they have. The Word of God, when received in real revelation, will bring faith, but often the Word cannot be received with proper revelation unless we also carry out the Word concerning fasting. Then the quickening power of God's Spirit quickens things to us by powerful revelation in such a manner that FAITH shines forth in outbursts of radiant action. We can claim all of the promises that are applicable to us for which we are burdened.

48. Fasting is a power behind DIVINE HEALING, behind the develop-

29

ment of the fruit of the Spirit, and the receiving of the gifts of the Spirit. No Christian can be at his best, without seasons of fasting and praying.

49. Fasting is a preventative for backsliding. Prayer alone is not always the preventative.

50. Prayer and fasting are the best antidotes for national corruption.

NATURAL REASONS WHY WE SHOULD FAST

There are many, many more reasons WHY ONE SHOULD FAST. We have just touched very briefly upon the most important SPIRITUAL REASONS. Please remember that in the above mentioned statements, we are referring only to the CONSECRATION FAST. This is the fast dedicated to Jesus by anointing ourselves with oil, or allowing the elders in the church to do so, where there is a group going on a fast. Matt. 6:17. It is a fast with much prayer, consecration, and yielding to the Lord. Jesus is very much pleased and honored when we come to Him, freeing ourselves from the natural. We exalt Him to the highest. Don't worry, you will be rewarded a thousand times.

We are again discussing WHY I SHOULD FAST, only this time we are considering the subject from the PHYSICAL STANDPOINT INSTEAD OF THE SPIRITUAL. Please bear in mind that any person, saved or unsaved, can receive the natural, secondary physical blessings of fasting, but only the consecrated child of God can receive the great spiritual blessings. When we go into food abstention, we give the stomach a vacation and vacate into the Spirit, then the tabernacle of the Holy Spirit goes into HOUSECLEANING. Cleanliness is Godliness. Nothing can clean the house of the Holy Spirit more effectively and quickly than giving our stomachs a HOLIDAY. If the physical side of fasting was all that was received by abstaining from food, it certainly would be worth fasting and people would live twenty-five to thirty-five years longer (according to health authorities). Many of God's people are committing "SLOW SUICIDE" by being continually on a three-meal-a-day stuffing habit, not satisfied with stuffing God and FAITH out of their lives, but go right on STUFFING OUT THEIR OWN LIFE YEARS AHEAD OF TIME. They stuff HEALTH OUT, AND INVITE DISEASES AND DEMONS IN. AFTER WEARING OUT ONE SET OF TEETH DIGGING THEMSELVES TO THE GRAVE, MANY SECURE ANOTHER SET TO FINISH DIGGING THEMSELVES TO DEATH.

We shall consider some of physical reasons

WHY FAST?—BELIEVE IT OR NOT

51. When you feed a diseased body you feed the disease; fasting starves the disease.

52. Fasting rids the body of all the poisonous filth of autointoxication and food decay.

53. Fasting improves the circulation. It even cleanses the blood vessels, so that blood circulates through the vessels that have heretofore been closed.

54. Fasting rests, improves, prevents, and overcomes heart trouble.

55. FASTING CONSERVES ENERGY. Sick people cannot get well unless there is a conservation of energy. Many times food will destroy or waste what little energy a sick individual has.

56. Fasting gives the overworked stomach a vacation, as well as nearly all other parts of the body.

57. Fasting rapidly removes the cause of many diseases.

58. Fasting will cure 99% of all functional ailments.

59. Fasting quickly heals simple diseases such as boils, skin blemishes, indigestion, dyspepsia, auto-intoxication, constipation (although at first the fast seems to aggravate the condition), rheumatism, fever, anaemia, poor blood, asthma, change of life and irregular periodical functioning in females, restoring to normal, and healing various other diseases. Long fasting will also cure most of the major diseases caused by impurities in the system. Barren women are often able to have children.

60. Fasting is the greatest blood purifier known.

61. Fasting eradicates mucus, stringy, ropey fecal material, and floating food particles from the intestines.

62. Fasting usually makes an individual stronger day by day, after the first ten or fifteen days of fasting.

63. The headache generally felt while fasting, is a sure indication that we *should fast.*

64. Fasting will remove ordinary headaches, including the coffee or caffeine headache, as well as the over-used coffee drinking HABIT, if one does not invite it back after the fast.

65. Fasting will also eradicate tobacco, drug, and drinking habits, in about seven to ten days. The roots of these habits are imbedded within the stomach. Fasting consumes these very roots.

66. A person cannot starve while fasting. During the fast the very things that are not needed within the body are used. Some of these are poisonous, contaminated, rotten food particles that have been on the walls of the stomach for months. This very condition invites disease and DEMONS, and by fasting they are starved out.

67. Fasting is the greatest youth restorer known.

68. Regular fasting prolongs life from twenty to forty years, depending on how frequent and how long the fasts are.

69. Fasting will remove tumors as large as melons, also ulcers, cancers, and goiters, arthritis, heart trouble, nervous diseases, tobacco, alcohol, drug and other habits, and will revitalize the glands.

70. Fasting causes one to become weak at first, because the rubbish and poisons within the body are being brought to a head like a boil; it is sorest when it is brought to a head, before the core is removed. The weakness while fasting generally disappears after the worst poisons and pollutions are removed by the housecleaning process. A person becomes stronger day by day.

71. Fasting, after two weeks, more or less, causes the breath that was so

foul during the first of the fast, to become clean and pure like that of a child's.

72. Fasting removes the bad taste and unpleasantness from the mouth.

73. Fasting will so purify the skin that often the complexion becomes rosy like a child's.

74. The older a person becomes, the more often he should fast. No one becomes too old to fast. History and the Bible show us that the men and women who fasted the most, lived the longest. Study Moses, whose "eye was not dim, nor his natural force abated" at "an hundred and twenty years," (Deut. 34:7), and Anna, the prophetess, who "served God with fasting and prayers night and day" and "she was of a great age."

75. Fasting overcomes many bad habits, and aids in restoring to normalcy the functions of our body.

76. Fasting develops patience, and aids temperance.

77. Fasting aids in the *prevention of disease.*

78. Fasting draws the intestinal tract to its normal size, and overcomes and prevents colitis.

79. Fasting restores a natural, normal appetite, after the fast is properly broken. The stomach being smaller, requires less food, saves much money.

80. Fasting is for thin, underweight people. Many times a thin person will point to a heavy person, saying they need to fast, and not realize that in most cases the thin person needs the fast more than the heavy person. The reason is very simple, THE THIN INDIVIDUAL HAS MANY TIMES SO OVERWORKED HIS ORGANS BY OVEREATING, THAT HE IS INCAPABLE OF PUTTING ON WEIGHT. I have seen many an underweight person fast from two to three weeks, and weigh more after breaking the fast properly, than they weighed before fasting. A heavy person is usually in good enough health, so that his organs can put on weight.

81. Fasting is a normalizing agent; it will help to restore weight to underweight folk, and aid in preventing excessive weight on overweight folk.

82. Fasting will aid in cases of insomnia, although at first *an automatic blood transfusion* is set up within the body caused by the blood remaining in the body from the weight that is lost. This excess blood goes through the body to bathe the organs, and it enters into the head causing sleeplessness for a time. Later on, and after the fast, one finds rest and sleep easier and more refreshing.

83. Excess starches and sweets cause the body to be converted into an ALCOHOLIC FACTORY. Alcohol is manufactured from them, and this in turn causes HABIT HUNGER, which is LUST HUNGER, and is entirely different from true hunger. There are perhaps more people bound to this habit than there are to the drinking habit. The former is about as difficult to break. Jesus classifies it as just as much of a sin as the drink habit. Luke 21:34. FASTING WILL UNDO THE HUNGER HABIT OF LUST, AND WILL PREVENT FOLK FROM BEING DRUNK ON FOOD.

84. Fasting should be frequent, to clean the temple of the Holy Spirit.

85. Fasting aids and improves our sight, hearing, taste, touch and smell. All sense faculties are benefited.

86. Fasting improves the mental faculties, making it easier to think, study, remember, and concentrate more efficiently. (During some parts of the fast, at first, this may not always be true.)

Fasting seems to take one into a different world. It is wonderful to taste and experience a new life. It makes better harmony, for the person, his family, friends and community.

88. Fasting is a tremendous power, whether it is used for God, or for ourselves. Individuals, whether Christians or not, who have fasted for their own career, vocation, skill or "labors," will have results. But when a fast is performed for our own personal purpose, the Scripture informs us that we will not have our Father's reward. We may have our own reward, or the reward of man. ("In the day of your fast ye find pleasure, and exact your labours." Isaiah 58:3, 4; also Matt. 6:16-18).

89. Heathen people in other lands fast many days, and many weeks, to demons and to the devil, and by their fastings are able to do exploits. They attribute their power to their fasting to these evil spirits. And many times these exploits are miraculous, and of greater power than many Christians are able to do without fasting. How much more should the children of God accomplish in performing supernatural things, through fasting and prayer. It puts us to shame when we think of the multitudes of suffering and dying humanity.

90. Fasting is a natural, tremendous and spiritual force. It can be used for God, for ourself, or for Satan. We would recognize this and should be the more willing to fast for Jesus.

91. According to some Christian physicians, there is no habit or weakness, that can survive a siege of fasting and prayer.

92. Fasting enables one to conquer self desires, and the habit of masturbation. Col. 3:5 and Rev. 2:7.

93. One of the worst of habits, yet one that is not considered very bad, because it excuses itself under the good name of tasty food, is nothing more than the well-nigh universal *stuffing habit*. A surfeiter is placed first, and the drinker second. Luke 21:34, "Overcharged with surfeiting and drunkenness." And see Matthew 24:38, "In the days that were before the flood, they were eating and drinking." Fasting breaks this habit of stomach-stuffing.

94. A good thing is disguised in order to give a front and an excuse for the indulgence in same. Satan delights in having God's people sin in a way that they think it is not sin. There is a record in God's Word of more people destroyed at one time from over-eating, than from getting drunk with alcoholic drinks, believe it or not. (Read Psalm 78.) The biggest sin of our Lord's people, is their continued stuffing His Spirit and power out from their lives. This is one of the contributing causes of self-righteousness. This habit weakens our moral fibre, and often leads to worse habits, such as the

alcoholic habit. The next thing following self-righteousness is that the individual becomes bound to some denomination or preacher. If the preacher does not follow God's pattern properly, the follower also is led astray, often being led into false doctrines. Rom. 16:17-18. With the oil lost from their lamps they become the class of foolish virgins the Bible speaks about when Jesus returns. Fasting is a remedy for surfeiting, and a good preparation for our Lord's return.

95. Fasting not only keeps our natural appetites subdued, but the natural appetite of eating is delivered from habit hunger, so that we eat what we need instead of what we lust after.

96. Fasting is the ladies' best beautifier; it brings grace, charm, and brings into normalcy all female functions. (While on the fast they may become temporarily abnormal.)

97. Fasting is the best method for developing self-control in all things. It gives us control over anger, impatience, nervousness, restlessness, and sharpens our mental facilities.

98. There is more in the Bible about long fasting than short fasting and long praying.

99. Fasting is considered both the quickest and greatest curative agency known to man, outside of divine healing.

100. Some of the most successful people in all walks of life are those that put God first and pray and fast.

A world-wide revival will surely begin as saints of God take up the burden of travailing prayer while fasting. Please send in names and addresses of your friends, and free sermons and literature will be mailed to them.

CANADIAN FASTS FORTY DAYS IN ZERO WEATHER

Dear Brother Hall:

Greetings in Jesus' name. I am just breaking my 40-day fast and really feel fine. Praise God, I was *never hungry during the whole fast*. I felt fine all the time, and was always up and around, inside and outside where the temperatures have been below zero this winter here in Saskatchewan.

I was fasting and praying for a revival among the saints of God.

BONDAGES BROKEN
I feel this has been the *greatest experience of my life* and many bondages have been broken in my life. I have a freedom that I never had before. Please send me the following tracts . . .

Thanking you, I remain,

Dave W. Siggelkow, 708 19th Street, West, Saskatoon, Sask,, Canada.

DAVID'S FAST

All Christians are delighted to read the Psalms; they encourage us to press onward. They are filled with scores of promises and blessings for believers. The Psalms are a product of Fasting and Prayer. The sublime utterances in the Psalms are not exaggerations, as has been asserted by some. Only in the realm of higher receptivity made possible by prayer and fasting, is the soul able to receive such revelations as Psalms 35:13; 69:10; Psalm 78:18-32; 107:17-18 and 109:22-26; II Sam. 12:16-23.

David sought God in long fasts; in fact he fasted so long at times, that he looked like a skeleton. Psalm 109:23, "I am tossed up and down as the locust. My knees are weak through fasting; and my flesh faileth of fatness. I became a reproach unto them: when they looked upon me, they shaked their heads." So much fat was lost that he actually became a reproach to look at; his friends and neighbors shook their heads. No doubt some ceased to be his friends and began criticizing; this is just what happens today when an individual seeks GOD long enough in fasting and prayer. Some people say we should always go into the desert or wilderness to fast, like Moses and Christ. That is good, but here is an instance in which David did not care who saw him. (This fast is also prophetical of Christ's 40-day fast.)

David must have fasted forty days or longer, to have lost so much weight. David was not interested in what people thought of his appearance. He fasted in mourning and humbleness; he was only interested in how he could please God, and reach HIM. I have seen many folk who fasted longer than forty days, yet they looked better than this description of David.

As certain as we "labor for the meat above," we shall not stand in very high favor with the world. When we enter into the spirit of fasting and prayer, we are not interested in what others say about us. We are after that which is worth more than silver and gold. If you fast and pray, and really get into the spirit of it, your prayers may seem more difficult at times, than when you are praying without fasting. The main victories are usually attained after fasting. In the battle you are progressing further, with higher mountains to climb, darker places to penetrate, higher walls to surmount, and deeper depths to plow through. (See Chart No. VII, Hindrances and Obstacles.) Psalm 35:13: "I humbled my soul with FASTING; and my PRAYER RETURNED INTO MY BOSOM." Fasting is not something to glory in, or to be puffed up about. Along with the fast we are to go down into humility, disregarding what people think and say. It should be a time of real weeping and mourning. Our unworthiness should be realized, and the farther down we go, the higher will our Christian experience rise. It will be a great spiritual fight all the way through.

I wish to state that some children of the Lord fail to press into the proper place of prayer, along with the fast, just because they find it difficult to pray. But that is no reason for not praying. Your prayers will absolutely blast through to heaven, if you settle down to do it, and labor at the job, and "ask" and "seek" and "knock," as Jesus told us to do. The Devil will be around to hinder, and prevent you from accomplishing your purpose, but PRAY THROUGH, FAST THROUGH, and press your way through till you open heaven. Shorter prayers under the influence of fasting, are far more effective than longer prayers when off the fast. We are in a channel of prayer, while fasting, that leads directly to the throne. The ear of God is open to hear the prayer of His fasting saint.

Usually, the first few days of a fast are the most difficult time to pray, because the weakness of the body has not gone, and the body has not been cleansed. Pray as much as possible, as long as possible, and as fervently as possible, regardless of lack of strength, and when you get over *"the hump,"* it becomes easier to fast and pray; generally speaking, you get stronger physically. You can gradually put yourself into it, devoting more time to prayer; then the fast itself actually becomes prayer. Please bear this in mind when fasting. A Christian then has such power, that these obstacles mentioned will seem easier and easier to surmount, as one presses on to more and greater obstacles, all of which will be victoriously overcome, and a continual growing power, greater than ever, will be felt by the person, as long as he or she stays in the center of God's will.

Those employed, or who are are working at various jobs, will find it difficult to spend all the time seeking God in prayer. But you can still secure very desirable results, and the Lord will bless you much, if you can keep in a spirit of prayer while you work. If one's work is extremely burdensome, it will be difficult to fast and concentrate in prayer. Sometimes a person on a job has begun a fast, and a time of prayer, and has become so lost in the spirit of prayer that nothing matters but Jesus Christ, and they lose interest in their work, and everything else around them, to such an extent that they receive a special call of God for their life work.

Some years ago, a shoe cobbler did this very thing. He was living in Denver, Colorado. After fasting and praying for forty days, the power of God became so real and precious, that he gave up **"FASTS 40 DAYS. MARVELOUS MIRACLES."** his shoe business, started preaching on the street corners, and blessing sick people through the healing ministry of Christ. Hundreds of sick people were prayed for daily, and many miraculously healed. Blind eyes were opened; deaf ears were unstopped; deaf and dumb spoke; ulcers, cancers, arthritis, and tuberculosis cases, were gloriously healed. The lame leaped for joy. Wheel chairs, beds, crutches and braces were left behind by the ones that were healed in Jesus' name. All this in answer to the prayers of an individual who caught a revelation through prayer and fasting for forty days.

Every minister owes it to his congregation to be at his best; every evangelist owes it to the people in each revival; every teacher owes it to his pupils; and every Christian to his brethren, to be at his best spiritually; and we have seen that this can only be attained through prayer with fasting. Prayer becomes illuminated, and fasting makes prayer as powerful as dynamite.

SHOULD I WAIT FOR GOD TO LAY A FAST BURDEN UPON ME?

No, not necessarily, for the simple reason that if we waited for God to lay a fasting burden upon us, there probably would be no fasting, or very little. Fasting is like praying. We pray when there is a need, without waiting for a burden of prayer. We should also fast when there is a need, and because it is our Christian duty. In Mark 2:20, Jesus has already laid a fast upon us in these words, "Then shall they fast in those days."

36

Chapter VI

THE FOUR APPETITES

Humanity is confronted with four appetites. One or more of these major appetites can get the best of us, if we allow them to do so. Intemperance and extreme indulgence can so easily overcome us if we fail to maintain self-control. The Bible admonishes us to be "Temperate in all things." The four appetites are:

1. THE SPIRITUAL APPETITE   3. THE APPETITE OF SEX
2. THE HUNGER APPETITE   4. THE APPETITE OF GREED
                                                (Covetousness)

The appetite of hunger will be discussed first, as it holds the key to the other two. Food stimulates both sex and greed.

The lust of sin can be gratified in one or more of these appetites. Three of them are carnal or worldly, while one is religious or spiritual. Even a sinner has a spiritual or religious nature, regardless of whether or not that sinner serves the true and living God.

It was through yielding to temptation that Eve gave way in satisfying her "desire" nature, by gratifying these same appetites. The temptation of Jesus Christ was similar to Eve's temptation, and it was exactly these same four appetites through which Satan chose to tempt Jesus. First, hunger—"Command that these stones be made bread." Matt. 4:3-10. Did Jesus please Satan and yield to the appetite of hunger by using His spiritual power to perform a miracle?

The spiritual appetite intercepts the natural appetites in the way and manner in which these are gratified.

SEX APPETITE

When a person tries to commit suicide or kill another, or tempts God along the line of suicide or murder, we find that it is related to the sex nature, as sex and death, or life and death, are kindred. Through our creative forces God gives us life and health, and also our offspring that we love.

The ancients, and the Magi, and the wise men of the Bible, so considered the creative forces of man to be related to death. They, too, knew that an individual with an irrational sex nature sometimes had a suicidal mania, and also that sex was one of the contributing causes to ruthless, bloody crimes of torture and killing. The life giving forces of nature can be used as a blessing, or misused for destructive purposes.

In the zodiacal sign, "Scorpio," which is the eighth sign of the Zodiac, we have a picture of a scorpion with its stinger lifted ready to strike. This is the sign of death, and is supposed to govern the sex area. Just before this sign in the heavens, there is a sign of the Judge, Jesus, who is the

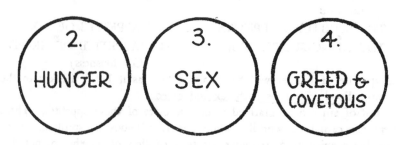

THE FOUR APPETITES BEFORE FASTING

CHART No. V. The spiritual appetite is insignificantly developed, compared with the three natural appetites. This is the way the average Christian appears to God before fasting. It explains why it is so difficult for a person to obtain the necessary SPIRITUAL PROGRESS in their life without having the natural carnal appetites subdued first. Fasting is the key, and almost the only process that guarantees the complete conquering and mastering of self, and the desire nature, so the full manifestation of the power of God will be made available. "NOTHING SHALL BE IMPOSSIBLE, BY PRAYER AND FASTING." The body is now the servant of the soul. Fasting has mastered this body; God is within our reach, and Heaven is opened.

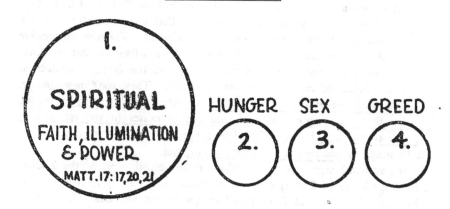

No. VI. THE FOUR APPETITES DEPICTED AFTER FASTING

CHART No. V. Note that the spiritual appetite is highly active and developed at the conclusion of a protracted fast, compared to the appetites of hunger, sex, and greed (covetousness). The love of food is "THE SECOND ROOT OF ALL EVIL." In a major fast HUNGER IS ABOLISHED after several days, and with it every desire of Sex, and later on of Greed. All NATURAL DESIRES LEAVE, and as far as the faster is concerned, he has none. Then, and then only, can an individual be receptive and empty enough to receive the greater things and the spiritual gifts of God, which come to us by FAITH. Prayer becomes intensified, fasting becomes prayer, and the individual reaches a spiritual height with God that is possible in no other way. "God is a Spirit, and they that worship Him must worship Him in Spirit and in Truth." John 4:24. For more details, see the author's 224-page text book on the subject, "THE FASTING PRAYER," containing many illustrations.

---

giver of LIFE. Jesus proceeds toward death and pulls the STING OUT OF DEATH. "O, death, where is thy sting? O, grave, where is thy victory?"

Likewise, today among students, it is generally understood that the creative forces of man are kindred to both life and death in the natural. However, it is not difficult for any of us to understand that the proper care of the creative physical forces of man leads to long life, and the improper abuse of them is a speedy way to the grave.

When Satan tempted Christ, "Then the devil taketh Him up into the Holy City, and setteth Him on a pinnacle of the temple, and saith unto Him, 'If thou be the Son of God, cast thyself down: for it is written, "He shall give His angels charge concerning thee: and in their hands they shall bear thee up, lest at any time thou dash thy foot against a stone" '." Matt. 4:5, 6. Satan's rage knew no bounds. Jesus Christ was now coming into the full manifestation of His sonship. He was now prepared to begin His ministry. He had won the victory. Satan had previously failed to destroy Christ, when He was a baby, through King Herod; now Satan sought to overcome Him by these temptations. Satan was trying to get Christ to do something foolish; this temptation could have been a means of suicidal destruction. No! Satan did not destroy Jesus here, for Jesus did not yield to this temptation.

It is very important that the reader have these four appetites fixed firmly in mind. A clear understanding of them will give one a richer knowledge of the Bible, and a better understanding of the purpose of fasting. A more vivid understanding of the whole temptation of Christ will be clearly seen. We also are tempted through these same appetites.

The covetous appetite of GREED, which is No. 4, was perhaps Satan's trump card. His greatest offer to Christ was to "show Him all the kingdoms of the world, and the glory of them; and saith unto Him, 'All these things will I give thee, if thou wilt fall down and worship me'." Matt. 4:8, 9. The appetite of covetous greed is an appetite of abnormal desire. Desire for

39

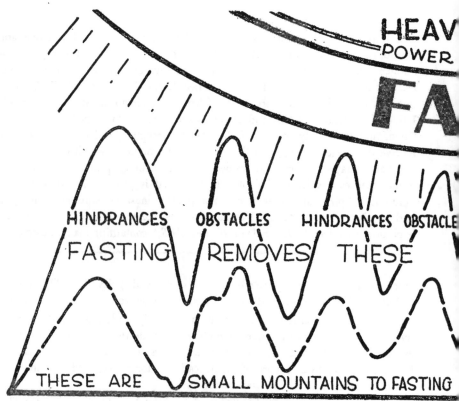

HINDRANCES   OBSTACLES   HINDRANCES OBSTACLE

FASTING   REMOVES   THESE

THESE ARE   SMALL MOUNTAINS TO FASTING

CHART No. VII. Illustrates THE BIG MOUNTAINS THAT ARE REMOVED BY "FAITH" THROUGH FASTING AND PRAYER. They may seem very difficult to move by prayer alone. "HAVE FAITH AS A GRAIN OF MUSTARD SEED, YE SHALL SAY UNTO THIS MOUNTAIN, *REMOVE*, and IT SHALL REMOVE TO YONDER PLACE." Matt. 17:21, 22. The recipe for this is, PRAYER, FASTING and PRAISE.

---

possessions, property, money, wealth, power, or for any kind of worldly possession, even for clothes. These desires, when placed above our love for God, turn the covetous appetite into sin. All of these appetites are normal in their proper places. Here, as in the two other major temptations, Satan was calling on Jesus to use, or rather misuse, His Spiritual appetite to worship Satan himself, in exchange for the kingdoms of this world. Many, sad to say, have sold out for worldly possessions.

The possession of these kingdoms and power would lead to the gratification of the desire—of greed. He could have had possession of these kingdoms, had He yielded to the greed nature. This, thank the Lord, He did not do —Satan was badly defeated. Satan did have it in his power, then and now, to offer Christ the kingdoms of this world, because now he is "the god of this world." But Satan is a usurper. His power will not last for long.

40

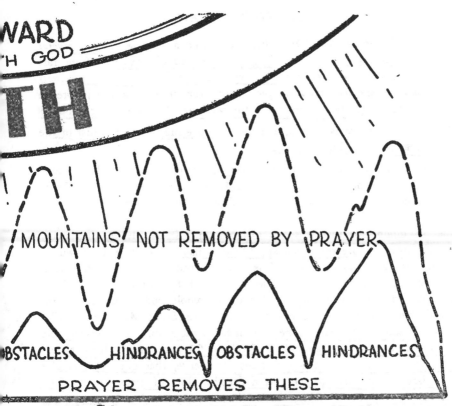

WARD
H GOD

TH

MOUNTAINS NOT REMOVED BY PRAYER

OBSTACLES HINDRANCES OBSTACLES HINDRANCES

PRAYER REMOVES THESE

The lower mountains represent answers to many of our prayers. The dotted lines in background represent our UNANSWERED PRAYERS THAT CAN BE MOVED "BY NOTHING EXCEPT PRAYER AND FASTING." "Whosoever shall say unto this mountain, Be thou removed and be thou cast into the sea; and shall NOT DOUBT . . . he shall have whatsoever he saith." Mark 11:23; also Mark 9:29. Fast! Praise! Believe! Confess it!

In Revelation 5:7, we see Jesus rising from the right hand of the Father, and taking the title deed to the world, the "book." Soon Satan will be evicted from the heavens and the earth, then Jesus' throne will be set up.

Thus the four appetites of man have been shown herewith, so that we can better realize what happens spiritually, when we fast. Every person has these four appetites. Perhaps one or another is more intensified in some respects —more intensified than is shown on the chart "before fasting." But, nevertheless, whether or not we realize it, the spiritual appetite is insufficiently developed, compared to the carnal appetites of the flesh.

Christians with everyday cares of business, job, and home, are usually so out of tune with the spiritual realm, that it seems practically impossible to get into communion with God. Therefore they are not in a position to contact God about the major problems of their life, without fasting and praying.

41

Now herein lies a WONDER that seems like a miracle. *After several days of the fast have passed, the hunger appetite actually leaves.* If the fast is prolonged, in a few days, possibly a week or ten days more, *the weakness leaves, and the average individual feels even stronger* than he did before he began the fast. (It takes longer for the weakness to leave older people.)

The next thing that is noticed, and this is noticeable during the first of the fast, is that appetite, No. 3, sex desire, leaves.

Then, finally, as the one who is fasting proceeds to pray and commune with God, and earnestly seeks the God of Heaven, the greed appetite No. 4, or the appetite that is the over anxious driving force which causes man to work hard at his job, and worry over his home affairs and his business, becomes so diminished that it seems insignificant. It usually requires many days of fasting before the greed appetite diminishes. This explains why a long fast is sometimes necessary. The chief interest now is in seeking God in prayer and fasting. One becomes indifferent to natural things. It is wonderful when one is glorifying God in his whole body, soul, and spirit, with all his members focused toward heaven. As Sister Mary Sommerville writes, "It was so wonderful I never wanted to eat again. The unspeakable glories of heaven were all around me; I felt as if I were sailing all the time." So glorious an ecstasy is this marvelous experience, that our every faculty can at last be extended toward heaven for the glory of Jesus Christ. The precious Holy Spirit may at last have His way with our lives in every way and detail. We hear His voice, as our spirit is attuned to heavenly things.

If God's people could for one moment realize what a tremendous thing this fasting truth is, there would be thousands more who would fast. As a result, we would see major miracles performed, and a great NATIONAL REVIVAL. The dead would arise, demons would be cast out, thousands of incurable diseases healed, all in the name of Jesus. Will you do your part?

Now your attention is called to the chart, showing the appetites *after* a fast (Chart VI, four appetites after fasting). Notice that appetite No. 1 takes predominance over the other appetites. Our entire nature seems to be loosed from the clutches of the natural, and we take on a new environment. We see the Body of Christ as one. We are no longer bound.

Heavy trials and tribulations will be present, and many burdens and obstacles seem to come across our pathway. At times it seems that there is a wall against us which our prayers cannot penetrate. Do not be discouraged. If you do not give up, certain victory lies ahead. You are in a great spiritual battle. At other times while praying, it will seem that you are in heaven. Visions and revelations from God may be yours.

Generally speaking, fasting will be a heavy, burdensome experience, because Satan does not want you to obtain the great "FAITH" that is promised to who fasts. You will be fighting against spiritual forces of darkness.

Chapter VII
THE FOUR GREAT ESSENTIALS

There are four things necessary to human life. They are placed herewith in order of importance:

1. THE FIRST GREAT ESSENTIAL TO LIFE IS AIR, NOT FOOD.
2. THE SECOND IS NOT FOOD, AS SOME WOULD SUPPOSE, BUT WATER.
3. THE THIRD, IS STILL NOT FOOD, BUT SLEEP.
4. FOOD IS THE FOURTH GREAT ESSENTIAL.

Of the four great essentials, food is generally put first, because we have to pay for it; while air, water and sleep are available on a "when-needed" basis, without cost.

For illustration, little animals, tested in the laboratories, have taught us some interesting things. These animals, deprived of food, but not water, for twenty days, lost more than half their weight, yet were afterwards saved by judicious feeding. But when they were completely deprived of sleep, even while getting more careful feeding and other attention, they died within five days.

The human being reacts similarly. In a protracted fast, extending into weeks of time, a person can rest and sleep properly, and come out feeling fine. *The longest period of authentic wakefulness on record is not quite ten days.* Legends of prolonged insomnia are heard from time to time, but as they have never been verified, they continue as mere legends; consequently, food is proven to be less important than sleep.

Food is less important than water because a man in a hot desert sun will die in a few hours, or several days at the most, if he has no water to drink; (this is more fully explained elsewhere). Food is less important than the air we breathe, because, if we could not breathe, thereby getting fresh air into our lungs, we would die in a few moments. So food does not have as important a place in life, as most of us are inclined to believe. Although a person can continue weeks, and sometimes even months, without anything to eat, which is much longer than he could live without any of the other essentials, yet food has a very important place in the physical welfare and is one of the four essentials. Please see the chapter following this one on how long a person can fast. We have just shown how important, in their respective order, the FOUR GREAT ESSENTIALS are to the physical man. There are other essentials, for the SPIRITUAL LIFE OF MAN, that far overshadow the above mentioned physical essentials.

THE FOUR SPIRITUAL ESSENTIALS

The greatest of all ESSENTIALS for man is THE LORD JESUS CHRIST. He is our ETERNAL LIFE. In HIM we have "THE BREAD OF LIFE," which is the source of all essentials. This is our FIRST ESSENTIAL.

(2) The second great spiritual essential is the Baptism of the Holy Spirit. He is for all believers. "Have you received THE HOLY GHOST SINCE YE BELIEVED?" (Acts 19:2.) "The Holy Ghost fell on them, as on us at the beginning." "And God, which knoweth the hearts, bear them witness, giving them the Holy Ghost, even as He did unto us." So IMPORTANT AN ESSENTIAL IS THIS THAT IT *IS* A COMMANDMENT: "Commanded them to wait for the promise of the Father."

(3) The third great essential is also from our Lord. This is Spiritual DIVINE HEALING, in answer to the prayer of FAITH. See James, chapter five. If we do not have enough FAITH to obtain healing, it is definitely pointed out in Mark 9:29 that the reason why we do not have FAITH is because we do not FAST with our prayers: "By nothing, but by prayer and fasting." One reason FASTING is not understood, is because it is so nearly like FAITH. It is the very threshold of faith itself.

(4) The last GREAT ESSENTIAL for the believer is: JESUS MUST RETURN "SO THAT THE DEAD IN CHRIST SHALL RISE, AND WE

Chart No. VIII.

TIME REQUIRED FOR HUNGER AND WEAKNESS TO LEAVE

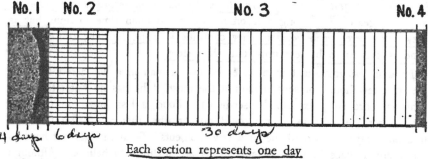

Each section represents one day

CHART SHOWING THE FOUR PHASES OF FASTING ON A 40-DAY SCALE:

1. DARK AREA: APPROXIMATE TIME REQUIRED FOR HUNGER TO LEAVE.
2. SHADED AREA: APPROXIMATE TIME REQUIRED FOR WEAKNESS TO LEAVE. (IT MAY TAPER OFF.)
3. LIGHT AREA: THE FAST PROPER; FASTING IS ROUTINE HERE, AFTER THE BODY IS CLEANSED.
4. HUNGER RETURNS AFTER A COMPLETE FAST.

Note: With different individuals the time may vary greatly in respect to the length of each phase. It may be shorter, or longer. The contrasts may be greater in young people, than in older persons. The average is shown.

AVERAGE AMOUNT OF EFFORT REQUIRED IN FASTING

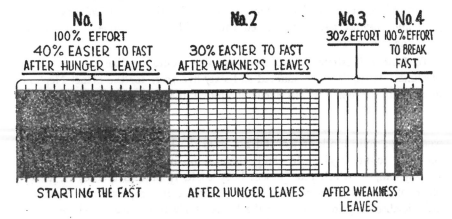

CHART SHOWING THE PERCENTAGE OF EFFORT REQUIRED IN TAKING A PROTRACTED FAST. (FIGURES ESTIMATED ONLY.)

1. IT REQUIRES 100% EFFORT AND WILL POWER TO GET STARTED. SOMETIMES SEVERAL ATTEMPTS WILL HAVE TO BE MADE. THE FIRST DAYS ARE THE MOST DIFFICULT. Do not be discouraged if you have to make many attempts.
2. IT BECOMES EASIER TO FAST AFTER HUNGER LEAVES.
3. AFTER WEAKNESS LEAVES, FASTING BECOMES ROUTINE AND IS NOT NEARLY SO DIFFICULT.
4. IT REQUIRES AS MUCH EFFORT TO BREAK THE FAST PROPERLY, AS IT DID TO BEGIN THE FAST.

WHICH ARE ALIVE AND REMAIN SHALL BE CAUGHT UP TO-GETHER WITH THEM IN THE CLOUDS, TO MEET THE LORD IN THE AIR: AND SO SHALL WE EVER BE WITH THE LORD." I Thess. 4:17.

Before MAN can be adapted to the spiritual realm, and see Heaven, he must be born again, and be like Jesus Christ. He cannot enter heaven in his present bodily condition. Supreme Intelligence designed the human body for the physical conditions of the planet "Earth," and it is perfect for that environment. It would be just as much out of order for worms to live in the air, and birds to live in the earth, as for man to live in heaven without

---

For more complete treatment, please consult Author's other four books. (All books different). *"THE FASTING PRAYER," "GLORIFIED FASTING," "BECAUSE OF UNBELIEF,"* and *"OUR HEALING OBLIGATION."*

45

this new birth. Man's natural body is not designed for life in heaven, or life on any other planet. Suppose you should desire to go to the neighboring planet, "Mercury." You could not take your body there, as it is seven-tenths fluid. Water boils at 212 degrees Fahrenheit, and Mercury, being so near to the sun, has a temperature of 750 degrees Fahrenheit! In a couple of hours you would be buried under a stone with this inscription: *'Well done! thou good and faithful servant.'* Indeed you would be well done. You would be burned to a crisp.

To further illustrate, let us see what life would be like on the planet Neptune. It requires one hundred and sixty-five years for the planet Neptune to make the complete zodiacal circuit around the sun; that is, one year on Neptune equals one hundred and sixty-five earth years. The temperature is about 400 degrees below zero, Fahrenheit! In less than thirty minutes you would be a solid block of ice, and not even the heat of Mercury could thaw you back to life again. In short, there is no other heavenly body in our solar system, on which your present body could remain alive. Lack of atmosphere, absence of water and food, and difference in temperature and gravity, make it absolutely impossible for the human body to survive anywhere except on the planet Earth. How could your natural body live in Heaven, as Heaven lies far beyond our solar system?

The NEW BIRTH now, and a glorified body later, IS THE ANSWER. "When this mortal shall put on immortality," we shall possess a glorified, redeemed body, fitted to live in the glory of heaven.

The four Gospels and the Epistles teach these fundamental spiritual essentials. It is the main teaching of Jesus Christ and the apostles. Fasting and prayer will enable us to more fully realize them, and appropriate them into our lives.

The four Spiritual essentials come to us through GOD in HIS THREE-FOLD PERSONALITY, PLUS THE *MAN* NATURE THAT JESUS CHRIST TOOK UPON HIMSELF THAT MAN MIGHT BE REDEEMED; they are:

1. GOD THE FATHER   4. GOD THE MAN
2. GOD THE SON   (THE SON OF MAN)
3. GOD THE SPIRIT   Jesus became man as well as God.

FOR A CLEARER PICTURE, please see CHARTS X and XI, THE BODY RENOVATED (MAN DIAGRAMMED) and THE WELLS OF LIVING WATER, in the next chapter.

This leads us to the FOUR ESSENTIALS OF MAN (AS A CHRISTIAN):

1. BODY   4. NEW BIRTH or the
2. SOUL   "NEW MAN," LIFE
3. SPIRIT   ETERNAL

THE FOUR ESSENTIALS OF UNREGENERATE MAN:

1. BODY   3. SPIRIT
2. SOUL   4. D E A T H

46

The above sets of fours, and many other Bible fours, would make an interesting and unusual study:—The four horsemen of the Apocalypse, of Revelation 6; the four horns of Zechariah 1:18; the four carpenters of Zech. 1:20; the four chariots of 6:1; the four beasts of Daniel's vision; and the four living creatures of Ezekiel's vision (chap. 1), that stand "before the throne" (Rev. 4:6) and cry "Holy, holy, holy, Lord God Almighty."

Chapter VIII

HOW TO FAST

Speaking of food, one does not realize the huge quantity which is consumed in the course of a month by an ordinary individual, until one fasts. Most of the American people consume far too much food. According to health experts, the American people as a whole suffer more or less with auto-intoxication. The Scriptures show us plainly that we should be temperate in all things. A study of Psalm 78, along with other Scriptures, shows us vividly how much God dislikes the glutton. "So they did eat and were well filled: for He gave them their own desire. They were not estranged from their lust. But while their meat was yet in their mouths, the wrath of God came upon them." "He gave them their request but sent leanness into their souls."

Some people wear out one set of teeth digging their way to the grave. Then they buy a second set to finish eating themselves to death.

William Penn, the founder of Pennsylvania, has said concerning temperance: "To this a spare diet contributes much. Eat therefore to live, and do not live to eat. That's like a man, but this below a beast."

It is very important to point out here for emphasis, that fasting and starvation are two entirely different things. Fasting is a physiological process. Whereas fasting is beneficial, and will rid the body of most diseases, starvation is detrimental, and if continued long enough, ends in death. (This could seldom ever happen, before approximately one hundred days.) The difference between these two processes is fundamental.

The appetite of hunger will have to be overcome and overruled for the time being, with extreme will power, and assistance from the Lord. The first days of the fast are very, very difficult. Sometimes several attempts will be necessary before the candidate will have fasted long enough for hunger to leave. Not only does the body crave food at stated and regular times, by reason of long-continued habit, but the mind likewise becomes restless and continues to remind one that food would be relished. The battle is both mental and physical.

One never realizes until he begins a fast, how important a factor food really is, to his mental frame of mind, as well as to his physical and spiritual being. As long as the body is continually nourished, one does not think of food to

47

any great extent, but as soon as it is withheld, it begins to occupy an important part in the mental life; one has a constant tendency to think of food. He anticipates, even at the very beginning of the fast, the day when abstinence will terminate, and when eating will again become possible. This craving of the body can be overcome only by immediate distraction to other activities, and by keeping in the spirit of prayer. A glass or two of water will alleviate the immediate gnawing symptoms, which usually develop in the region of the stomach. These sensations are produced by the rhythmic activity of the muscles in and about the stomach, and are present when food is first withheld, and when the thought of food occupies the mind. As soon as this thought is banished, by concentration upon Christ, these rhythmical muscular contractions (known as the *peristaltic action*), soon subside. After a short time, these acute sensations of hunger will pass away, probably to occur again later, perhaps at the next regular meal time. A repetition of the water drinking, and prompt distraction of attention, will again dispose of these symptoms. After three or four days, it will be found that real hunger will not return again until the return of natural hunger at the conclusion of the fast. Habit hunger, which is different, will often make its appearance, and leave just as unexpectedly as it came.

SALT WATER FLUSH

If one wishes to hasten the effects of fasting at the beginning, a salt water flush can be used to flush out the colon. (This should NOT be used after the first several days.) To one quart of hot water, add two level teaspoons of salt, and drink. This may be done at any other time on an empty stomach, when not fasting, for cleansing purposes.

Very often during a fast, one will become highly sensitive to the taste of water. The taste sense becomes very acute, as well as all of the senses, and one will detect flavors and metallic tastes never noticed before. Bottled, or other pure water, is preferable to ordinary hydrant water.

"DRINK WARM WATER" To avoid cramps in the stomach, and some other unpleasantness, hot or warm water should be drunk instead of cold water, unless the cold water is taken very, very slowly. This is more important if a person is thin, or the fast taken in cold weather.

One of the greatest obstacles to be overcome by practically all who undertake this unusually beneficial experience, will be the persuasion of over-solicitous relatives and friends, who invariably endeavor to tempt him to break his fast prematurely, on a false alarm that he is injuring his body, or he is starving to death! These persuasions of over-solicitous relatives become very strong and insidious, and he may fall by the wayside, and give in to a tempting dish. If he does, he should not be discouraged, because frequently many efforts, and much will power, will have to be exerted.

A common belief that one must remain indoors, and perhaps in bed, throughout a fast of any duration, is entirely erroneous and is based on the assumption that we derive our strength and energy directly from the food consumed. A certain feeling of languor may be present during the early or latter days of a fast. A working man can continue working if his work is not overly strenuous. His prayer, however, will not likely be as concentrated, or as effective. Sylvia McVay writes on her 42-day fast: "I did all my housework, cooked three meals a day for my husband and four children, washed our clothes on a washboard, and attended church every night."

Before arising in the morning, one should exercise gently in bed and breathe deeply. This will counteract any dizziness and any other strange feelings that may occur at first. Plently of water should be taken; this should be taken slowly. Usually these symptoms are felt during the first few days only, and disappear entirely later on (When hunger returns, the weakness experienced will be real and will not pass away as the earlier symptoms did). Never rise from any position suddenly. The purpose of rising slowly is to get the blood in free circulation, so that you will not experience fainting.

After the body toxins have been consumed, eliminated, and oxidized, one will feel stronger mentally and physically. Pains, dizziness, weakness, and peculiar feelings, will have disappeared. All of the various organs and parts of the body, as well as the sense faculties, will be revitalized. Spiritually, one will feel as if the demons of hell are turned against him. It is doubtful if you will ever have such trials as the strange ones that show up while fasting, or at the close of the fasting period. The trials encountered at this time are numerous; naturally, the Devil will fight to prevent a child of God making headway toward FAITH. It simply means defeat for Satan. Jesus' greatest testing came *after* He had fasted forty days and forty nights. BEFORE HE PERFORMED A SINGLE MIRACLE, HE FASTED. FASTING AND PRAYER DRIVES OUT ALL UNBELIEF AND DOUBT. Read Luke 4, Psalm 109:22-31, and Psalm 35:13.

You will be rewarded. THERE IS NO SUCH GRAND, GLORIOUS, and WONDERFUL EXPERIENCE IN ALL THE WORLD, AS THE MARVELLOUS VICTORY BROUGHT BY PRAYING AND FASTING. WORDS CANNOT DESCRIBE THE BLESSINGS. PRAYERS THAT YOU HAVE BEEN PRAYING FOR YEARS, WILL BE ANSWERED. YOUR DISEASES, OR THE SICKNESS OF OTHERS THAT YOU HAVE BEEN SO LONG PRAYING ABOUT, WILL DISAPPEAR. Your loved ones will be saved. You will have power, and answers to prayer that you never before dreamed were possible.

Although various complications, many of which have been enumerated, appear while fasting, such as fainting, fever, dizziness, headaches, a tendency to vomit, severe sharp pains in the abdomen, weak knees, short breath, sleeplessness, or sleepiness all the time, nervousness, vexation, foul breath, watery nose, sneezing, backache, burning kidneys, sideache, etc. THESE DO NOT all appear at one time. PERHAPS ONLY ONE OR TWO may be noticed by any one individual in an entire fast. Please do not be alarmed, as this is just a natural result of the fast, and in nearly all cases is experienced

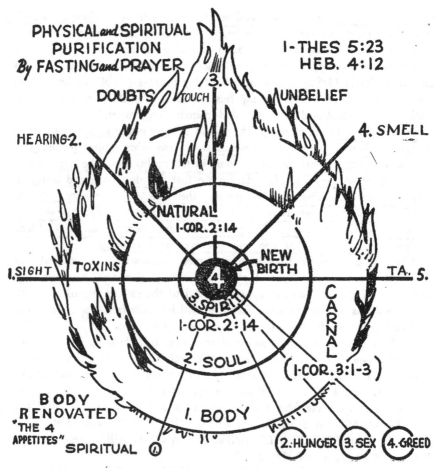

CHART No. X. THE BONFIRE
MAN ANALYZED AND DIAGRAMMED

The vital energies are freed from the laborious task of digesting, and pushing food material through thirty feet of tubing, not to speak of the energy required for increased rapidity of heart action. Just as soon as all of this energy is released by abstention from food, OXIDATION BEGINS WITH-IN THE BODY, which IS NOTHING MORE THAN A BONFIRE IN WHICH ALL OF THE WASTE POISONS ARE CONSUMED.

The (1) body, (2) soul, (3) spirit, and (4) new birth, are depicted, together with the five sense faculties of (1) sight, (2) hearing, (3) touch, (4) smell, and (5) taste. It is pleasing these sense faculties that leads to the gratification of the four appetites (see bottom of chart), that prevents the child of God from obtaining the better things. The natural appetites are larger than the spiritual appetite. But turn to the "Wells of Living Water Chart; "after the holy fast," and note that the appetites are reversed.

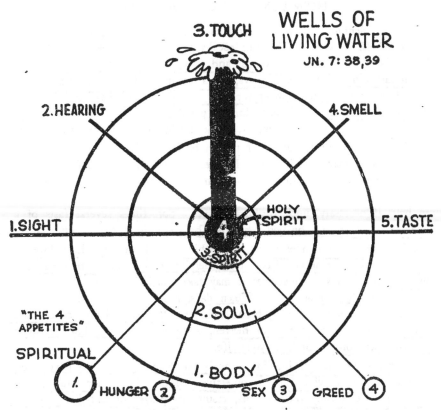

Chart No. XI. The SPIRITUAL MAN ANALYZED AND DIAGRAM-
ED AFTER FASTING AND PRAYING. NOTE THE BAPTISM OF THE
HOLY SPIRIT IN THE HEART OF MAN WHICH IS THE SOURCE
FROM WHICH THE "WELLS OF LIVING WATER" SPRING. ALSO,
HIS FIVE SENSE FACULTIES ARE DIRECTED BY THE HOLY SPIRIT
FROM THE SOURCE OF POWER THROUGH FAITH IN CHRIST.

THIS REPRESENTS THE IDEAL MAN, WITH ALL THE APPETITES,
all the members, and the body, soul, and spirit completely yielded to the
Lord for service. This man will "LOVE HIS APPEARING," and will be
looking forward to the great change that will take place in him when the
"Trumpet sounds." He has an abundance of the oil of the Spiritual anointing.

---

only during the first part of the fast. Usually hot water drinking, enemas
and exercise will stop the condition. After the body is cleansed, the condition will subside. Pains in abdomen are often caused by drinking cold
water too fast. A change to hot water will remedy the condition. Oxidation of waste material in the intestines causes the *fever*. Large enemas
wherever necessary, are helpful. The enema bag should be elevated high.
Some medical advisers, however, state that it is not always necessary for
the bowels to move when fasting—that enemas are not always necessary.

HOW LONG SHOULD WE FAST?

Until we definitely know that God has heard our prayer, so that we can acquire "THE POWER" that Jesus speaks of, to do the seemingly "impossible." We should continue to fast and pray, regardless of whether or not this requires one meal, seven days, or a complete fast of several weeks, forty days, or until true hunger returns, which usually takes several weeks, or sometimes longer. It is our glorious privilege and duty to fast through to a victorious experience. However, we do not buy God's favor by this work.

It is more difficult for an older person to fast, although from a physical standpoint they may need it more. It takes a much longer time for weakness to leave; sometimes fainting tendencies may be felt, and due to this condition, it is advisable that an older person be with another individual, who can help if necessary, until weakness leaves. Sometimes several fasts of a week or ten days may be better at first, before a long one is undertaken.

A few days after hunger leaves, or within a week or two, depending on age, the weakness that you have felt generally leaves, and fasting becomes much easier. (In some instances it may take much longer.)

After these first eight, ten or fifteen days, more or less, fasting becomes a matter of routine and actually becomes easier. You should now concentrate in prayer, seek an answer from heaven, a revelation, a healing, or some spiritual operation of God, in your life.

After fasting and praying for what is God's will for us to have, then discontinue your praying for the objective sought. Continued praying for things that are already promised us, results in prayer of unbelief. Those prayers are not answered. Please lay claim on it now, by fixing a time for your faith to explode, and from there on, always thank Jesus for it. You will be a possessor. From now on "confess it." Study carefully Romans 10:9, 10. This Scripture applies to anything we may want from God.

PASTOR FASTS TEN DAYS AND 300 CONVERTED

MEN ARE LEARNING HOW TO RECEIVE GIFTS

Dear Brother Hall:

June 14, 1949

Some time ago a friend sent me one of your books, "Atomic Power with God." I was only a little interested when I first received it, but it grew on me. The anointing of God was upon your message.

Just recently I fasted into my tenth day, and along with my Bible I kept your book near. The Lord met me in a wonderful way during this fast; however I was forced to quit far too soon. My pastoral work took up too much of my time. When I fast again I expect to take it during my vacation, so that I can devote my full time to waiting on God.

The above book was studied during a recent fast by a friend of mine. In ONE WEEK'S REVIVAL SINCE THESE FASTS, THREE HUNDRED PEOPLE WENT INTO OUR PRAYER ROOMS FOR SALVATION. I HAVE SEEN MORE OF

FASTING BRINGS. BIG REVIVAL

GOD'S POWER MANIFESTED, SINCE YOU HAVE WRITTEN YOUR BOOKS, AND MORE MEN LEARNING HOW TO GET HOLD OF GOD FOR SPIRITUAL GIFTS, THAN AT ANY OTHER PERIOD I KNOW OF SINCE THE TIME OF CHRIST.

Please send me your other books . . .

Yours very truly,

Pastor Harvey L. Smith   Box 262, Pascagoula, Miss.

Chapter IX

FASTING IN RELATION TO THE PHYSICAL BODY

Is fasting harmful to the physical body? This question has been raised more than any other question concerning the subject of fasting. In the light of modern medical science we can state with assurance that fasting is not in the least harmful. Fasting purifies and cleanses the body; it permits a balancing of the circulation, absolutely essential to good health; it allows the various eliminating organs to dispose of the effete material from the system, and to oxidize, or burn up, the useless matter which has accumulated, like ashes in a grate.

When a fast is begun, the first things which are oxidized and eliminated are those useless materials floating about in the form of mal-assimilated food material, which sometimes choke the small blood vessels and congest the lymph vessels. In other words, THE VERY THINGS WHICH WE WISH TO ELIMINATE FROM THE SYSTEM, ARE THOSE WHICH NATURE ACTUALLY DISPOSES OF FIRST OF ALL. Fasting is house-cleaning of the body. The Holy Spirit, then, is given a clean temple in which to dwell. Cleanliness is also godliness. When assimilation stops, the processes of elimination are greatly accelerated. We will show four methods used in this process.

THE FOUR MEANS USED IN HOUSE CLEANING

(1) The SKIN, through its millions of pores, is one channel through which much toxic waste is eliminated. Much more waste is removed through our pores during a fast, than at any other time. This is one reason Jesus said, "When thou fastest . . . wash thy face." It is also a good practice to bathe frequently to keep the excreted material washed away, and the pores open.

(2) The KIDNEYS: Much water drinking is so highly beneficial. It dilutes the urine which constantly washes out the poisons that are poured into the kidneys. Water drinking is a "MUST," during a fast. Drink at least six glasses of water daily, or enough to satisfy thirst.

(3) The LUNGS play an important part in this house cleaning process. It would seem almost unbelievable that loads of poison are exhaled in the fast through the nostrils, from the oxygenation of the blood. The same amount of poison is released through the nostrils and lungs, as through the kidneys, bowels and skin. All persons smell alike during the first part of the fast, and a person familiar with fasting will recognize the odor as that of a brother or sister, fasting, and instead of criticizing, will rejoice in his or her heart that his brother or sister is fulfilling some of the works of the Lord. If a person is praying and fasting as he should, the odor will not bother him. If you do not wish to have an obnoxious breath around your

neighbor, get some menthol crystals at the drug store.' A very fine crystal particle will dissolve on the tip of your tongue, so that your breath will not be noticed for a long time; there will be such a small amount in the tiny crystal, that it will not get back of your tongue far enough to get into the stomach. The reason that I mention this point, is that some folk have chewed gum when fasting, and the amount of sugar in the gum would be almost enough to break the fast. The menthol crystal will be stronger than gum, more lasting in the breath, and too small to reach the stomach. This is only a suggestion. Bad breath is a good sign that the house cleaning process is going on. This vapor that comes from the lungs will clear up later on in the fast, and the breath, as well as the taste in the mouth, will become as CLEAN AND ODORLESS as that of a baby, believe it or not.

(4) The BOWELS are the fourth channel of elimination. It would be well if they would move every day or two, but often they move with less frequency while on the fast, but do not be alarmed if they should not move very often.

Since all four of these methods of elimination are at work, is it any wonder that fasting is a way towards health? If in good health, this is a method for preventing sickness.

Fasting is the most powerful, and the quickest agent known, for curing functional ailments. Especially is this true of stomach disorders. That is why it is so very necessary to break the fast carefully with fruit juices, followed by fresh fruit, for several days.

If a person is in an adverse state of health, his eyes, throat, liver, glands, blood, and a little later even his kidneys become REJUVENATED and greatly benefitted. This is a natural law, designed of God, and this physical aspect is touched upon so that we may realize that fasting and prayer to God is harmless to the body. Would it not be unreasonable to think that Christ would ask us to fast, if it would hurt us physically? We have a good God, and He asks us to do nothing that will hurt or harm us. One can FAST for a long period of time, and secure GREAT SPIRITUAL RESULTS WITHOUT BODILY HARM, and in addition receive much physical benefit.

If one is afraid that he is harming himself, and full of fear, he cannot obtain the best spiritual results from the fast. The Lord certainly does not want us to come to Him in fear, but rather in a spirit of trust. Fear is one thing that must absolutely be dismissed from the mind entirely.

IS FASTING STARVATION?

Absolutely not!

Fasting and starvation are two entirely different things.

To illustrate: The complete fast begins at the time you omit one meal, and it ends after a large part of the body weight is lost, usually when true hunger returns (Matt. 4:1-4). It may last several weeks or longer. Jesus' fast lasted forty days, before true hunger returned: "He was afterward an hungered." In His fast, He fasted naturally, just as you or I would. When a man has a KEEN APPETITE, and is really *hungry* at the end of a long fast, as Jesus was, it is an indication of good health. Any physician will tell you that a man with a good appetite is in good health.

At the end of a complete fast, hunger sets in; at this point starvation begins, if the fast is continued after true hunger returns. It was when starvation had just begun, at the end of Jesus' fast, that the devil sought to take advantage of the hunger, by tempting Him. Satan fears to see God's children fast with prayer, because it means his quicker defeat. Fasting is like "dynamiting" Satan.

Starvation begins after most of the body weight is lost. It usually starts after true hunger returns, which is seldom less than twenty-one days, and may be as long as forty, or even sixty days. It is difficult to state the exact time when starvation sets in. It varies with different individuals. Fat people can fast much longer than thin ones, as the body can continue for weeks, living on the superfluous fat material.

The end of starvation is death. Death occurs when an individual has continued a fast long after true hunger has returned, and usually long after starvation sets in. Some confusion exists here. When you hear that someone died of starvation in a sea-wrecked vessel in two or three days, there is some mistake. A person might easily get cold, or become frightened to death, in a few hours time, or a few days time, but cannot possibly starve to death in such a short period if he has water to drink. He might also worry to death in a short time.

A human being is like a vital electric plant that is so constructed that it is ordinarily supplied with power from the dynamo, but may run for a considerable length of time on the battery current. For each of the millions of cells of the body is a cell similar to the most perfect cell of a storage battery. Fasting stops the dynamo, and automatically turns the switch to the battery current, which is just as capable of sustaining life as the current from the dynamo. The physically healthy individual has more storage capacity than one with a weak constitution.

In Yeo's *Physiology*, we find the longest case on record. "The patient, suffering from a gunshot wound in the abdomen, lived *four months without any food.* His weight decreased from 159 to 60 pounds.

LIVES 120 DAYS WITHOUT FOOD Every function was almost dormant. Thought was unimpaired; *the brain was unusally clear"* (this is always the case with anyone fasting) "and the brain was found to have suffered no loss in size." The percentage of decrease of different parts of the organism, including other cases considered, is given by Mr. Yeo:

FAT	97%	BLOOD	17%
SPLEEN	63%	LIVER	56%
MUSCLE	30%	NERVE CENTERS	0%

Note the zero percentage of decrease of the vital nerve centers, including the brain. Note particularly the 97% fat consumed, showing that the body utilizes as food the surplus fat which can readily be spared without injuring the organism. Do not these striking percentages indicate that the body is designed for fasting? that it is so created that it can survive a long foodless period without injury? Are not these figures a wonderful proof of the divine wisdom in creating and designing a body prepared to meet, and able to handle, the exigency of a long foodless period?

A human being cannot starve to death in several weeks of fasting if he has water. He can die if he worries to an extreme, or becomes overly frightened, either with food and drink, or without food and drink.

One should not drink milk or coffee when fasting for to do so is dieting and not fasting. Nothing at all should be drunk except water. It is a purifying agent, and is necessary to wash out the poisons from the system.

Unless one's work is unusually heavy, it is not necessary to give up his job. If he is not getting sufficient exercise in praying or work, he should regularly take exercise to assist the fast. It is then easier to fast, and very beneficial as well; the weakness leaves more readily and the fast gets underway more quickly. Exercise keeps the blood circulating. However, if we pray as we should, one will get all the action and exercise needed, because real praying is hard work, and this is what we need if we are to see great spiritual results. It is important to secure sufficient rest and sleep. If possible, take more rest when fasting, than when not fasting. More rest may be required, although one does not seem to miss sleep as he would while eating.

THE BIBLE IS AHEAD OF SCIENCE

The "blood," or "life" of the flesh is the last part of the body to be consumed after starvation sets in. It is at this point that a fast passes over into starvation. Credit is given William Harvey for his great medical discovery of 1615 A.D.: "The circulation of blood. Life is blood, or the circulation of blood." This is considered a great milestone in the history of medical science, but if you check into the Holy Scriptures, you will find that this is not a new discovery at all. Thousands of years before William Harvey's day, God told Moses this very same thing: "For the life of the flesh is in the Blood." Lev. 17:11. (See also Gen. 9:4 and Deut. 12:23.) If the Bible were studied along with science, the scientists of the day would be more up to date, and not be so often obliged to revise their theories.

THE BLOOD AT WORK

The blood, as you know, is driven by the heart, through the arteries, into the capillaries, where it nourishes and strengthens the body. It then returns, through the capillaries by another route, the veins, to the heart from whence it is drawn to the lungs. The blood starts on its arterial journey, bright red and rich, laden with life-giving properties. It returns by the venous route, poor, blue and dull, being laden down with waste matter of the system. It goes out like a fresh stream from the mountains; it returns as a stream of sewer water. In a fast, the returning stream is far more polluted than when not fasting. This foul stream returns to the *right* auricle of the heart. When this auricle becomes filled, it contracts, and forces the stream of blood through an opening in the *right* ventricle of the heart, which in turn sends it on to the lungs, where it is distributed by millions of hair-like blood vessels to the air cells of the lungs. The foul stream of blood is now distributed among the millions of tiny air cells in the lungs.

MARVELLOUS PURIFI-CATION PROCESS Air is inhaled and oxygen comes into contact with the impure blood through the thin walls of these hair-like blood vessels of the lungs, with walls thick enough to hold the blood, but thin enough to admit oxygen. When the oxygen comes in contact with the blood, a form of combustion, or oxidation, takes place, and the blood takes up oxygen and releases carbonic acid gas, generated from the waste products and poisonous matter which have been gathered up by the blood from all parts of the system. The blood thus purified and oxygenated, is carried back to the heart again, rich, red and bright, and laden with life-giving properties and qualities. Upon reaching the *left* auricle of the heart, it is forced into the *left* ventricle, from whence it is again forced through the arteries on its mission of life to all parts of the system. It is estimated that in a single day

OVER 4,000 GALLONS OF BLOOD PER DAY of twenty-four hours, 35,000 pints of blood traverse the capillaries of the lungs, the blood corpuscles passing in single file, and being exposed to the oxygen of the air on all sides If the air cells of the lungs were spread out over an unbroken surface, they would cover an area of fourteen thousand square feet. When one considers the minute details of the process alluded to, he is lost in wonder and admiration of our blessed Father's care and omnipotence and omniscience.

Considering the value that the lungs play in the cleansing of the blood, one should be interested in proper deep breathing and securing plenty of fresh air. More about this is found in author's booklet *"Because of Unbelief,"* see back cover. (This volume will show a person how to have tremendous Faith.)

First and foremost as a cause of disease, is the congestion of the blood with morbid waste material from the organs and tissues of the body. This thickened blood, surcharged with products of imperfect metabolism, finds itself unable to pass freely through certain parts of the body, which is so necessary for perfect health. The damming up of the blood in certain organs and tissues produces an engorgement, which interferes with the free and natural functioning of that particular part. There are few of the disorders from which mankind suffers in which this condition is not present; and it is no exaggeration to say that this is one of the principal causes of most diseases.

The condition is brought about in the blood stream by eating more food than the body actually requires. Excess food and insufficient exercise results in incomplete utilization of the food. It requires a lot of unnecessary energy to digest and eliminate and otherwise dispose of the surplus, unnecessary food.

Jesus calls it *"SURFEITING,"* Luke 21:34. This is one of the contributing causes of skin blemishes, boils, growths such as cancers and tumors, and diseases of the mucous membranes, such as tuberculosis, ovarian and womb disorders, and leucorrhea.

Consequently a cure depends upon the elimination of this congestion, and a readjustment of the habits governing eating, exercising, etc., so that the body may be freed from these encumbrances. The best way to do this, is to stop assimilation for a time by fasting. This is most effective in producing quick results. Both physically and spiritually, the results are so astounding that it is like a bird in a cage set free in the wide open.

In earlier ages man was used to satiating himself to the utmost, with the food at his immediate disposal, and gorging himself upon the fruits of conquest. In these modern days of plenty, food became so plentiful that the cravings of hunger were fully satisfied, and the cultivation of epicurean appetites became more and more a vice. Man has actually suffered in a greater degree from this superabundance than from the enforced hunger of scarcity, and the struggle to provide sufficient food.

Occasionally some soul has cried out in protest against sensual gratifications, but the mad crowd pays scarcely any attention. They have little heeded the words of our Master's voice and the teachings of the Scriptures. Nor have they sought the power of the Spirit, but have made the belly their God, and their bellies the graveyards of their souls.

Temperance will be more readily practiced by those who understand that good eating habits will bring about rapid physical and spiritual changes which make for immediate happiness both now and tomorrow. Fasting conserves tremendous energy that can be utilized in building up the temple of the Holy Spirit.

Other teachers, besides the prophets and Christ, such as Krishna, Buddha, and Mohammed, have awakened the minds of their followers to some degree, to the moral and ethereal desirability of control over sensual pleasures, the root of which is EATING.

WHAT MEDICAL MEN SAY

The earliest physicians were united in teaching that abstentious living was the key to good health. They advocated the denying of food to a diseased body. Through the centuries, thousands of teachers have come and gone, with their circles of disciples, who practiced fasting as a cure for disease, but there were few patients that took the treatment seriously from their physicians. Possibly because it seemed like a Utopian dream, too good to be true, or the regime to be followed too strict, and requiring too much will power.

Some doctors, and medical and health authorities have issued publications that clarify this science of fasting, from the standpoint of health and the cure of disease. Some of these writers on the subject are: Dr. Tanner, Sinclair, Dr. McCoy, Dr. Shaw Haskell, Dr. Dewey, Bernarr Macfadden, Dr. John

Cowan, Tilden Brook, Dr. R. Walter, H. M. Shelden, Carlson, and others.

Dr. Frank McCoy in his book, "THE FAST WAY TO HEALTH," states: "I have made a most exhaustive study of every method of cure, from mind cure to modern surgery and gland therapy, and I HAVE NEVER FOUND A SINGLE METHOD THAT COULD APPROACH EVEN CLOSELY, IN ITS RESULTS, THE BENEFITS WHICH COME FROM SOME FORM OF THE FASTING CURE." Some of these volumes can be secured from your library. Dr. McCoy treats his patients by fasting and dieting methods. He also prescribes a very long fast for some conditions, for disorders of both women and men. Most of his book gives illustrations and examples of his patients placed on a fasting or dieting treatment. If more physicians would practice his method of healing there would be less sickness.

Fasting has a distinct value in obtaining and retaining *perfect health.* In early times, Avicenna, the great Arabian physican, clearly sensed the value of fasting, since he often prescribed as long as a three-weeks fast for his patients, especially for syphilis and smallpox. Dr. Isaac Jennings, as early as 1822, employed fasting successfully as an aid in almost every kind of ail- ment which he treated.

Fasting has proven a divine aid to the body's own processes of self recovery. Fasting in ailments such as *asthma, hay fever, constipation, headaches, colds, skin disorders, arthritis and rheumatism, blood diseases,* and anything else along the line of *blood or functional diseases,* has proven almost a miracle of recovery. Benefits have been observed in *nervous and mental disorders, paraly- sis, semi-paralysis, neurasthenia,* and in some forms of *insanity.* (Please bear in mind that we are now talking about *natural* divine aids, and not *divine healing* in this section.) By FASTING AND PRAYER THE LORD WILL HEAL US OF ANY SICKNESS, REGARDLESS OF WHETHER IT IS 'INCURABLE,' OR NOT. This would be divine healing. Many incurable diseases in man are caused by demons. Demons cannot be cured. They must be cast out. It often requires prayer and fasting to do so.

When food is withheld, oxidation begins within the body. This is nothing more than a collection of refuse gathered for a bonfire, in which waste poisons are burnt up just as a person would gather up the trash in his yard and burn it up in his incinerator. THIS IS INDICATED SOMETIMES BY A FEVER WHICH SETS IN DURING THE EARLY STAGES OF THE FAST, AND BY HEADACHES AND OTHER SYMPTOMS. A testimony from Burbank, California, reads, "I was surprised at the awful poisons that came out of my body. We should fast often, if it is only to keep ourselves clean." (Consult Chart No. X, Man Analyzed and Diagrammed.)

Fasting gives the body a much needed holiday, a vacation in which to recuperate. It never occurs to most people that the body seldom has a rest from its ordinary labors. We overtax and overload all the organs with by-products of our wrong living, eating, drinking and thinking. We do not grant these millions of little cells which labor so incessantly for our physical well-being any rest, no not even a SABBATICAL REST. Most folk would be far better off if they would pray and fast at least one day a week. They would be stronger physically, and deeper spiritually. Most of the early churches, especially the Methodists, had at least one fast day a week.

FASTING DOES NOT REDUCE, BUT INCREASES THE ENERGY AND HEAT OF THE BODY by the combustion of the waste poisons by a process of oxidation, in which waste becomes the fuel for its own destruction and elimination from the body. The process of combustion becomes a source of added bodily heat for the faster's comfort, as well as a source of added energy, bringing about revitalization and restoration of health.

Fasting RETAINS THE YOUTHFUL COMPLEXION AND APPEARANCE. FASTING DEFERS OLD AGE AND KEEPS THE BODY

FASTING RESTORES YOUTHFUL ENERGY

YOUNG. Flossie Winsor writes from Triton, Newfoundland, "My flesh is taking on a natural, rosy, youthful color. I feel like a new person." An early old age is both a biological and mental abnormality. It results principally from accumulated impurities and deposits. Abstention from food will help to remove the accumulations, and thus defer the physiological process that brings on old age. *We are only as old as the number of dead cells we have in our body.* Fasting converts dead cells into food fuel. This explains why we look so much younger after fasting.

With the PHYSICAL HOUSECLEANING, GOES A MENTAL HOUSECLEANING. I have personally seen pessimism, gloom, discouragement, anger, grudges, fear, morbidity, despondency, worry, fussiness, mental tensions, perversions, vile and depraved thoughts, excitability, other forms of mental conditions, and bad habits disappear completely after the bodily purification is accomplished. Bodily purification leads to spiritual purification. Demons often feed on food filth and carnality; many times fasting unlooses them and makes a person free from demons and disease.

The health authority, Bernarr Macfadden, tells us "That the body intimately influences the higher soul-powers during a fast, I definitely know.

AMAZING TESTIMONY OF BERNARR MacFADDEN

Physical renovation and purification lead to spiritual renovation and purification. I have experienced a sublimation of the Spirit, during a prolonged fast, which is difficult to put into words. It must be experienced to be known. There is a spring to the step, a feeling of joyous release, of gladness which fairly overwhelms one. There is, too, an exaltion of spirit, a broad and more generous sympathy, love and understanding for all things and for all mankind, a feeling of well-being, and of peace with God, with one's fellowman, with the world, and with all things which are a part of our everyday living." If this is the exalted experience of a person interested in the physical welfare of individuals, how much more glorious should be the experience of those who would "specialize" in power and faith with God through fasting and prayer? It takes Jesus, however, to give eternal life.

Chapter X

THE PROPER CARE IN BREAKING THE FAST

It is very difficult to break the fast properly, but very important. The importance of breaking the fast correctly and wisely cannot be over-emphasized. If you wish to avoid unpleasant consequences after your fast, please use plain common sense, and pay strict attention to the following directions. Very often an individual takes a fast of several weeks, and gets along fine in the fast, but to his disappointment, has uncomfortable physical difficulties while in the process of breaking the fast. In practically all cases this can be traced directly to his impatience to begin eating his accustomed rations days and even weeks too soon.

If you have fasted very long, or have taken a complete fast, you will have practically a brand new stomach and it will have to become adjusted to food again. If you had your automobile engine overhauled, it would be necessary to break it in slowly for so many miles. If it were a major overhaul, you should run it at a lower R.P.M. much longer. The same rule applies to a new stomach.

I once had an airplane with an 80-hoursepower engine. I had it "majored" by an A. and E. mechanic. Before I could fly it, even at a low R.P.M., the motor was run, while on the ground, for about five hours. After it had been broken in sufficiently to fly, it was flown at low cruising speed for another five hours. These ten hours that were required to break in the engine, were broken down into short periods, so that the engine would be properly broken in safely. Our bodies are like the overhauled engine. The longer the fast, the more care it takes, before resuming regular diet. Our stomach must be broken in gradually, and time is required between periods for rest, and for the gradual return to normal of the assimilative functions.

In Bible days, the Israelites, the prophets, and the disciples of Christ, were acquainted with the dietetic laws of Moses, and the teaching of the prophets and Essenes, and knew about the hygiene necessary to break a fast. But today most people are ignorant of this information. In a long fast the stomach is new, like a child's stomach. And when you break a fast, it must be done properly, to avoid injuring the stomach. Our body is the temple of the Holy Spirit, and we should be careful to protect it from injury.

After true hunger has returned (in some instances, true hunger does not return), or if one finds it necessary and advisable to break fasting before hunger has returned, he should use only fresh citrus fruits. Oranges and grapefruits are the best to break it with. Fresh tomato juice is almost equally good. Grape juice from fresh grapes is very fine. Sauerkraut juice, if agreeable, is sometimes good for the second or third meal, after the fast is broken. If the fast is seven days or less, it can be broken with whole fresh fruit for two or three meals, and light soups the second day; the third day green vegetables, and your regular diet from there on. Even after a short fast of two or three days, one should avoid sitting down at the table to eat a regular meal, if he wishes to feel comfortable afterwards. But it is not so necessary to break this type of fast as carefully as a fast that has been entered into for many days. (Canned fruits are satisfactory when fresh fruits or juices are not available.)

If the fast has been very long, it will take several meals of fresh fruit juices, in small diluted quantities, to correct natural tendencies. Your regular diet should not commence, until at least the number of days have elapsed, equal to the number of days that you have fasted. For instance, if you have fasted twenty-eight days, you should have a gradual breaking-in period of twenty-eight days before you resume a regular diet. You should start out with fruit juices for several days, then fresh fruit for two or three days more, then light soups, not too milky, for another two or three days, and then green vegetables for a further period. Gradually, little by little, break into the regular diet.

Since much weight has been lost, the quickest way to regain it, is by drinking milk, after several days of the above-mentioned schedule. Small amounts should be taken at first, then larger and larger portions. CAUTION: Sometimes milk will cause the individual to bloat, as assimilation will be too great. If this should happen, or any other difficulty arises, it is because you are rushing the breaking-in period. The remedy is to eat less, or cut out some of the food. If necessary, go back to fruit juices or fresh fruit again. If very severe, go back to FASTING, and do not drink water. Take enemas often. This is a safe rule to follow, if any complication should develop during the breaking-in period.

NOTICE: *THIS IS VERY IMPORTANT*

Do not rush your stomach. The longer you wait to regain your weight, and the more slowly you get back to regular eating, the better will be your physical condition afterward. If you fail to wait long enough, you will undo much that has been accomplished physically.

We urge you, by all means to obtain our book, *"GLORIFIED FASTING."* This volume will give you more information on breaking the fast than any other volume available. We feel that every person who fasts should have it. It is called the *"ABC of FASTING."* 40 illustrations, contains a scientific treatment of the "Fasting Cure" road to better health.

Dec. 4, 1951—FUNDAMENTAL BIBLE AND TRACT SUPPLY
Vancouver, B. C., Canada

Dear Brother Hall:—I have loaned your literature around in our Nazarene church. The pastor preached sermons on fasting. I am on a major fast too. As a result a great revival has broken out. . . . I can use more literature in my tract work. . . . Thank you, Neil D. Cameron.

Chapter XI

FORTY FAITH FACTS ABOUT DIVINE HEALING

JESUS CHRIST THE SAME YESTERDAY AND TODAY AND FOREVER
Hebrews 13:8
Many Become Healed While Reading This Faith Message

What the author is stating in regard to Divine Healing will also apply to any other prayer objective or petition of our heart to God. If you will apply these faith facts to other desires of your heart, I can promise you upon God's Word of authority that you can have them.

1. Divine Healing has already been completely paid for by our loving compassionate Saviour. "He hath borne our griefs (diseases), and carried our sorrows (sicknesses): yet we did esteem Him stricken, smitten of God, and afflicted. But He was wounded for our transgressions, He was bruised for our iniquities . . . and with His stripes we are healed." Isa. 53:3, 5.

2. Jesus is more willing to heal us than we are willing to permit Him to heal us. He is just as willing to heal bodies as He is to save souls. Psalm 103:3, Mark 2:9.

3. Our SALVATION (atonement) is not fully completed when our soul is forgiven, if our bodies are not also delivered from sickness and disease. The greater deliverance of our body is at the time of resurrection —when Jesus comes.

4. Healing is in our salvation as the new birth, and the forgiveness of sins as much of salvation as divine healing. Salvation is a composite word incorporating many phases of redemption.

5. Diseases and sicknesses are placed on us by Satan. The word "affliction" in most instances in the Bible is translated—our trials, tribulations, and hardships. These were not redeemed by Christ, for us on the cross as were diseases and sicknesses. We may be chastened through trials, persecution, tribulations, etc.

6. In II Cor. 12:7-10, Paul gives us some facts concerning his "abundance of the revelations" that were given to him, perhaps, above all men. Verse seven reads, "And lest I should be exalted above measure through the abundance of the revelations, there was given to me a *thorn in the flesh,* the messenger of Satan to buffet me, lest I should be exalted above measure." We are given both the reason as to his thorn and also what the thorn was, and believe it or not, Paul's thorn in the flesh, was neither sickness of the body nor opthalmia—a disease of the eyes.

In every instance in the Word of God where a thorn is mentioned, we are told exactly what it was (Numbers 33:55 and Joshua 23:13). In II Samuel 23:6: "the sons of Belial shall be all of them as thorns thrust away." Without exception these thorns were personalities. Paul's thorn was a "messenger of Satan." A messenger is an angel, or in this instance an angel of Satan. The messenger or angel is called a person and is translated "he." There is no sex to "opthalmia," therefore it is not a him or a her.

7. The excuse for unbelief, using Paul's "thorn in the flesh" as one of the greatest excuses against divine healing, should actually be one of the greatest reasons why we should be healed. We should never tolerate a work of Satan when it is the Lord's desire to heal. Paul's buffeting by Satan's angel is described through his sufferings, persecutions, tribulations, and hardships—(which Jesus did not bear). But Jesus will not suffer that we should be tempted more than we can stand. I Cor. 10:13. Although these are enumerated many times at a number of places in the Bible, nothing is ever mentioned of Paul having a disease or sickness. Paul, a chosen vessel, had such an abundance of revelations and visions that it became necessary to permit a messenger of Satan to keep him humble.

8. At the time of Paul's conversion, he was blind for three days. He was completely healed of this blindness after fasting three days, by Ananias laying his hand on him, thus proving it to be God's will that he see perfectly. Acts 9:6-17. We therefore conclude, that it was God's definite will for Paul to have proper eyesight, then why should we try to blame our Lord for undoing His will by giving him opthalmia?

9. An outline of Paul's life was given to him through the prophet Ananias and nowhere is sickness or disease mentioned with which Paul would suffer. There are numerous descriptions of the sufferings of Paul given in the Book of Acts and also in his epistles. In the enumeration, Paul mentions nearly everything with the exception of sickness and sore eyes.

10. Some Bible scholars are trying to put more suffering to Paul than he deserves Paul had plenty of real hardship cases, trials, persecutions and buffetings by Satan's angel. Why should man try to place more sufferings on one, than God does?

11. The traditional teachings of many religious leaders, scribes and Pharisees of our day, teach falsely that Paul's weak eyes were glorifying to God, and we too, must be sick to glorify God.

12. When we know the will of God definitely, we are then in a place to receive an answer to the promise. We cannot get healing or anything from God when we are not certain as to the will of our Lord. Practically everyone gets healed, who realizes that God wants to heal them more than they want to be healed.

13. We cannot be healed and doubt Jesus' healing atonement. If we doubt what He has provided for us, we doubt Him, thus making Him a liar.

14. We cannot be healed when we are bound to traditional doubtful doctrines of men concerning healing.

15. Many folk are denominationally bound, and yoked. These folk cannot obtain healing unless they are set free, and realize there are just as good or better folk in other churches. This is called denominational unbelief.

16. Many folk cannot be healed because they fail to walk in the additional light God has given them, such as the receiving the Holy Spirit, or that of fasting and prayer, etc. Their rejection of His truth, is the same as the rejection of Him.

17. Most of the time sinners can more readily become healed, than Christians who have served God for many years. Sinners come in repentance, while so-called Christians come in their own righteousness, boasting how much faith they had many years ago.

18. Christians are to make new consecrations in faith and fasting to God once in a while. (Matt. 6:12). "Let him that thinketh he standeth take heed lest he fall." I Cor. 10:12.

19. One has to have confidence and respect in the instrument God uses to bring deliverance to us. If we talk against this instrument or the truth the instrument is bringing, if healed many times one will lose it through nothing more than gossip.

20. One cannot come for healing beating the air and be in the midst of confusion. Emotionalism may have its place, but noise and emotions do not represent faith or the power of God, and will not bring healing.

21. The more a person relaxes and rests in the Lord, the quicker he becomes healed.

22. We cannot usually obtain healing when we continue to beg for it. We must use the Word of God and claim it, thanking Jesus for same. We should not continue to ask God for things He has already promised us. II Peter 2:24.

23. When healed, our bodies are made a-new the same as our souls were. We have the same joy of victory and we should rejoice in the same manner.

24. It is just as possible to backslide from healing as to backslide from the salvation of our soul. The remedy is to do the same thing that we would do, to keep the victory of the soul. This is usually by praising Jesus and living consecrated spiritual lives.

25. We need to keep associated with believers of faith and power when applying to Jesus for the healing of the body. Many times we have to disband from our own religion, church, and friends in order not to be around *doubters*. The influence of skeptics and doubters prevents many a person from not only obtaining, but in keeping their healing. This also applies to other spiritual things from God. When Jesus went to raise the daughter of Jairus from the dead, there was so much doubt, He had to put them out before raising her up. Mark 5:40.

26. Prayer and fasting will neutralize the flesh to such an extent that a person will become a powerful conductor of both divine healing and spiritual power. Healing will be more readily received into the body.

27. When any person, whether believer or unbeliever, is healed by the Lord, it is a sign that his or her sins are forgiven them. "If they have committed sins, they shall be forgiven him." James 5:15. They should continue to carry out their works of salvation to continue with spiritual anointing.

28. If traditionalism was properly broken down and every person realized the full atonement as they should, everyone could be healed at the same time they became converted. Jesus paid the full price in His complete atonement for the complete body, soul, and spirit of man. In our city-wide UNION HEALING campaigns scores are converted and healed at one time.

29. Fasting and prayer has enabled us to enter the greatest period the church-age has ever seen. The great healing campaigns are wonderful now, and the Lord is healing all manners of sicknesses and saving multitudes. Far greater things are for us, however, than we have ever seen up to the present time. (John 14:12). We will have them as soon as more members of the body of Christ put into practice a teaching that is given to us all through the Bible and as is in Matt. 9:15, and Matt. 17:21.

30. Jesus suffered with pieces of metal lashed into His beautiful back for our healing, before He went to the cross to atone for our sins. We therefore should receive healing (if needed) at the time of salvation, if we are to carry forward the order of Christ's sufferings. Many Christians have not fully accepted Jesus. They have not accepted Him as their healer.

31. We are not giving to our Lord, what rightfully belongs to Him since He bought and paid for us, unless we believe Him for the healing of our bodies. This is our spiritual obligation like any other duty the Christian is to perform. (Exodus 15:24-26; James 5.)

32. If believers will not tolerate sin in their life as the work of the devil, how much less should we tolerate the works of sicknesses and disease in our bodies, since they are also the works of Satan? Both are a product of the curse of the Law. See Gal. 3:13 and Deut. 28th Chapter.

33. Faith for healing does not look for feelings but sees the invisible first before seeing the substance that is the evidence. (Heb. 11.)

34. Faith is not "seeing and then believing," but "BELIEVING AND THEN SEEING." Faith brings the unseen things into sight.

35. If God's "Word promise" is not "Witness" enough that He will heal, or supply the need, then it is doubtful if the witness we are looking for would be worth much.

36. When our "sense faculties" say that it is not done, we should still hold God's promises above them. Is our "sense evidence" more to be relied upon than God's true Word? Are we daring to give the Word of God the pre-eminence over our feelings? The Word of God says that after hands have been laid on a sick person, He shall recover. We advise the sick to dare to stand on WHAT GOD SAYS, RATHER THAN BY WHAT ONE FEELS.

37. When Jesus was here in the flesh, He recognized the evidence of the sense faculties, but He never permitted Himself to be dominated by them. He made His senses, His servants. If we are to be followers of Him, we should also make them our servants, rather than give heed to them over and above the Word of God. Faith and fasting do not like our natural senses.

38. Jesus so ignored the "senses" of the flesh that He pronounced the

66

lame, healed when they were still crippled, He pronounced the blind man healed and the lepers cleansed when it appeared they were still in their disabled condition. The fig tree being cursed still looked (according to all sense knowledge) like it was in a normal natural condition. The invisible death of the tree became visible evidence the next day.

39. Although sense faculties control the natural man here; we are obliged to see that faith controls us in obtaining spiritual things from Christ. Spiritually, our senses are at war with the spiritual man and the Word of God. We cannot allow them to contradict the Word of God. WE MUST LEARN TO IGNORE SENSE EVIDENCE THAT CONTRADICTS THE WORD. Practice along this line with fasting and prayer will eventually produce some of the greatest spiritual giants of faith the world has ever seen.

40. Give your sense evidence a vacation by fasting and then you can act on the Word of God. Sense knowledge then becomes a lie. The acting on the Word in our heart and not in our mind, is faith. The Father honours this Word and brings to pass His already provided blessings. To carry on our sense faculty ignoring campaign, we must then ignore our symptoms, refuse our pains that may in some cases linger for a while, and act as though you believe His Word is coming to pass. Stand firmly on promises that are applicable to your case and repeat one over and over until you burn it in your soul. Cover your needs with promises! Jesus said, "I am come that they might have life (this included life in the flesh also), and have it more abundantly." John 10:10. "That the life also of Jesus might be manifest in our body." If Jesus' life is in our body, we will have no sickness or disease in the body. "I wish above all things that thou mayest prosper and be in health, even as thy soul prospereth." III John 2.

Faith is blind to physical reason and physical conditions. While reason is nervous, excited, and troubled; faith is patient, relaxed, and calm. Faith just takes over and possesses. All believers can have faith-power to heal the sick and cast out demons. See Luke 9:1; Matt. 10:7, 8; Mark 3:14, 15; and Mark 16th chapter. It is necessary to be grounded on the Word of God and believe the Word of God to retain our healing. Others could have faith for our deliverance, but we might lose the healing if we did not also have our faith properly grounded in the Word. This explains why some healings do not last after we are healed. We could get our faith more on the person delivering us, than on Christ. We would be healed, but if our faith was not definitely established in the WORD OF GOD, there would be a possibility of the return of the ailment. We must have Faith in God. A powerful Scripture for you to stand on and go about your duties throughout the day is one pertaining to sick people. (Mark 16:18, "The Sick!") "They shall recover." "THEY SHALL RECOVER." *"THEY SHALL RECOVER."* Now say it this way, I SHALL RECOVER, I SHALL RECOVER NOW IN JESUS' NAME! NOW is also the day of (Healing) Salvation.

In Monterey County my brother, Delbert Hall, arranged for a union revival where many ministers from many denominations co-operated in the Youth

Center and the Salinas Armory. Many folk had been fasting and praying. Faith power was high. I announced a subject, *"Seven Bible Methods of Healing Today."* We demonstrated that folk would receive their healing by dipping their hand in water seven times and shout with victory, "Hallelujah." They only did what they were told to do by FAITH WORDS (see Mark 11:23). Another group were healed in Jesus' name, by touching a garment; another group would receive their healing by shaking hands with Brother Carral J. Hodges, Rev. Charles J. Coffey, Rev. Amos E. Sloan, Rev. W. E. Wilfong, or some other person, and say Hallelujah. They would be healed, Some were healed by telling them to go do something else, and when they did it, the thing they did helped to release their faith and they were healed. Some were asked to walk across the shadow of Rev. G. L. Townsnd or Rev. Ray C. Kelley. When they did so they were healed. Other methods were also used such as using anointing oil and many times laying our hands on the sick. All healings were done in the name of our Lord. We witnessed deaf folk, who could hear a watch tick. Scores of arthritis victims were healed and did not feel a pain afterward. Many with ulcers, cancers, and tuberculosis were delivered under God's mighty power. When they obeyed the words that we presented to them from the Bible and stated positive words of deliverance, they were all delivered.

FAITH PARALLELS FASTING

Faith cometh by hearing, and hearing by the Word of God. But in the Word of God Jesus has given us a more direct and specific pathway to the receiving of this FAITH. The disciples needed to fast in order to obtain faith to cast out certain demons. If we are unable to get victory over ordinary sicknesses and achieve certain prayer accomplishments without fasting, how much more should we fast, than the disciples? Surely this should spur us on toward fasting more than ever.

If faith is produced by following Jesus' instructions on prayer and fasting, then there surely is a close relationship between fasting and faith. Shall we analyze the subjects of FAITH and FASTING and see the relationship between them?

FAITH

1. Faith ignores the sense faculties of sight, smell, taste, touch, and hearing.

2. Faith ignores feeling.

3. Faith works with the invisible.

FASTING

1. Fasting wars against our members so that the senses, though keen in operation, are subjected to the spiritual.

2. Our feelings change to a spiritual environment.

3. Our miserable feeling during fasting comes while the flesh is being subjugated so that invisible spiritual power may be manifested.

68

FAITH	FASTING

4. Faith is on a spiritual plane.

5. "Faith worketh patience." James 1:3.

6. Faith is a substance: "Faith is the substance of things hoped for."

7. Faith is the evidence of the unseen; "The evidence of things not seen."

8. Faith ceases to be when the substance is made visible.

9. Faith is anti-carnal.

10. Faith is believing what is not seen by the natural.

11. Faith brings supernatural manifestation.

12. Without faith it is impossible to please God.

13. Faith brings spiritual power.

14. Faith is the victory.

15. The natural man dislikes to believe in God.

16. Christians find it difficult to believe Christ for their physical healing, which was bought for them.

17. Faith pulls down the strongholds of the enemy. II Cor. 10:3-5.

18. Faith operates on an invisible plane, exposing evil forces.

19. The more we exercise our faith the stronger we become in our Christian experience.

20. Faith will make a supernatural person out of an ordinary individual.

21. Faith works independently of the flesh, and of all sense evidence.

---

4. Fasting leads us into the Spirit.

5. A major fast always gives one greater patience.

6. Fasting brings one into contact with the substance of God.

7. Fasting brings revelation evidence from God.

8. After the fast ends there is a major spiritual awakening.

9. Fasting is anti-carnal.

10. Fasting takes one into an unseen spiritual realm, sometimes into visions.

11. Fasting will undo the natural. It brings us into the supernatural.

12. Fasting pleases the Lord.

13. Fasting produces the faith that leads to spiritual power.

14. Fasting moves God to give us the victory.

15. The natural man dislikes to fast.

16. The children of the Bridegroom are urged to fast, yet it is so distasteful to them that seldom can one be found who has fasted ten consecutive days.

17. Fasting brings us into a great spiritual battle that ultimately brings great victory. See Daniel 10:2-14.

18. Satanic forces struggle against the fasting candidate, seeking to break the fast.

19. Fasting empowers a Christian to make great spiritual strides. To be at our best, we should be "in fastings often."

20. Fasting neutralizes the flesh so that a person can become a *powerful CONDUCTOR of Spiritual Power.*

21. Fasting is disliked by the flesh. The natural is restrained—God comes.

22. Faith surprises the flesh and overrides it with spirit power.

22. Fasting is an anti-flesh measure giving the flesh a beating.

23. Faith disregards the natural appetites and sometimes gives us supernatural appetites.

23. Fasting arrests the appetites so that they become dormant after three days.

24. Faith can be a fruit of the Spirit and a gift. It is one of the most blessed graces of the Spirit to practice and develop in order to please God.

24. Fasting and prayer can do more for a person, and bring that individual more closely to God, than can any other spiritual exercise. It therefore honors and pleases our Jesus.

Following Brother Branham's campaign in Calvary Temple (Rev. LeRoy Kopp, pastor), I was conducting salvation-healing meetings. A Sister Winkleman from Santa Monica had choking cancer so bad that her physicians gave her only thirty days to live. Mrs. Winkleman came to the meetings and began fasting. After commanding her to claim her healing in Jesus' name, every pain left immediately and in two days she vomited it up. She brought her skeptical husband to Calvary Temple who was astounded by the recovery. He had broken ribs that never did heal properly and was an unbeliever. During my message on faith he raised his hand to heaven while seated, and accepted Jesus completely for his body and soul. Immediately he was healed and saved from his sins. Later on that week Mr. and Mrs. Winkleman brought their three sons to the revival. One son was twenty, one was eighteen, and the third son was sixteen years of age. All three sons accepted Jesus as their Saviour. The whole family was converted and healed. This all came about while Sister Winkleman fasted ten days. She had been praying for several years for these deliverances, but when she fasted and prayed God heard her prayers. One month before, her sister had died with a choking cancer. I recently met her in Los Angeles and she is still healed today, nearly a year later.

CHOKING CANCER HEALED

The author was conducting a county-wide healing campaign with Rev. H. T. Owens and a group of other ministers and churches in Kern County. In this meeting many had been fasting and praying. There was such faith-power to accept things from God, all I had to do was to simply declare words of faith unto them concerning their deliverances. When I stated they were healed if they would rise and say Hallelujah, they were healed. Scores of healings from all manner of sickness were done in Jesus' name by nothing more than speaking words—words that were anointed by fasting and prayer. I seldom found it necessary to even lay my hands on them or anoint them with oil. Words were spoken and folk were healed at every service, the same way at a distance from me.

KERN COUNTY HEALING CAMPAIGN

For additional information on healing and FAITH, please order the author's volume called, "Our Divine Healing Obligation." Price .50.

Chapter XII

RESULTS OF FASTING AND PRAYING

St. Paul has probably inspired more men and women to follow Jesus Christ than has any other person. His teachings are more revered and loved in the church today, than are those of any other writer. After Paul's conversion he began his career with a three-day fast, Acts 9:9. If every convert would follow Paul's example by fasting three days, meditating and praying after his conversion, there would be fewer backsliders and more chosen vessels for the Lord's service. According to Galatians 1:17, Paul then went to Arabia, "Neither went I up to Jerusalem to them which were apostles before me." Preparation had to be made; Christ had to be woven into his theology. Changes had now to be made. A mystery is supposed to cover his stay in Arabia, but of the effect of fasting on a man of Paul's character, there remains no mystery. Since he says of his Christian career, he was "in fastings often" (II Cor. 11:27), there can be little doubt that he fasted in Arabia, when all the circumstances were most favorable for a fast. The result was that he returned to Damascus and began to preach Christ in power and demonstration of the Spirit. He became a spiritual giant for God. All of us need to go into "THE WILDERNESS," or "INTO ARABIA" BEFORE BEGINNING TO PREACH CHRIST. If there is that something lacking in your life, even if you have the Baptism of the Holy Spirit, the FASTING EXPERIENCE is for you. There would be more success instead of so many failures in the ministry. The power and demonstration in the Spirit would be manifested and gifts of the Spirit would commence to operate. If there is any one agency that can do this quickly and perfectly, it is the consecration fast. It is the sure route to the anointing.

We have been too busy with "much serving" as ministers, and have missed the power for the highest service, because we have failed to follow Brother Paul in his fasting as he has invited us to do when he says: "Walk as ye have us for an example;" surely, since he was "in fasting often" this is included in the example. In II Cor. 11:23 St. Paul says: "Are they ministers of Christ? I am more"—largely because he was "in fast-ings often." All of the verse, II Cor. 11:27, reads: "In weariness and painfulness, in watchings often, IN HUN-GER AND THIRST, IN FASTINGS OFTEN, in cold and nakedness," is herewith quoted to show that Paul distinguishes between doing without water in his hunger, and fasting, which is doing without food only, but not without the drinking of water. Here is the secret of being more than a mere minister. It is the secret of Paul's power. All who will take his words to heart can excel by using this glorious agency. We are obligated to do so to be our best.

PAUL WAS "IN FASTINGS OFTEN"

71

This command: "Be followers of me, as ye have us for an example," Phil. 3:17, is for all believers as well as for ministers like Paul. This is still more evident from the manner in which he refers to fasting and prayer in I Cor. 7:5,

MARRIED PEOPLE SHOULD GIVE THEMSELVES TO FASTING

"Defraud ye not one the other, except it be with consent for a time, that ye may give yourselves to fasting and prayer." These words cannot be construed as being addressed alone to ministers. They are addressed to all and it is a routine work of salvation that needs to be worked out after we are converted. Verse Six: "I speak this by permission, and not of commandment," pertains to the marriage relationship and applies to the sex appetite which should be denied in fasting. After approximately three days in the fast, the desire will have disappeared anyway. If the married couple wish all the happiness there is in wedlock, before you ever argue with one another about breaking up, try the fast way, and to your surprise things can be healed so that you will want to go on another honeymoon! Try it out and see. It is an inexpensive method, a money saver!

In Acts 13:1, 2: "They ministered to the Lord and FASTED." The result was finding the will of God. Paul and Barnabas were to be separated to the work whereunto God had called them. It seems that the Holy Ghost has little place in the churches in these modern days; but give the Holy Ghost a chance to lead through fasting and praying and see the results.

II Cor. 6:1-5: "We then approving ourselves as the ministers of God in much patience . . . in fastings." Surely, if he could not approve himself a minister of God without fasting, how can the rest of us presume to do so? Paul certainly was acquainted with the value of this tonic.

Ministers can be their own evangelists after a season of fasting and prayer and will do more good than a stranger could possibly do without fasting. There will be less psychology and fewer stories, but more spiritual power and demonstration, as well as fervor and zeal in the revival.

Bible students can obtain the choicest post-graduate course in the university of the Spirit by uniting for a season of prayer and fasting. They can become better commentators on the Pauline Epistle by obtaining the Pauline FERVENCY and ZEAL than they ever thought possible, by just following Paul's example.

We hold Bible conferences, fellowship meetings, basket dinner gatherings in the church, feasting, jubilees, musical services, and prayer meetings. Why not have fasting-prayer, and consecration-fast anointing services and conferences? The results have been astounding in the places where they have been held, as we shall presently tell you.

After Jesus received the Holy Spirit, although He was the Son of God yet He did not begin to manifest His Sonship until *after He had fasted forty days.* As children of God we will need to follow Jesus in fasting and prayer, if we expect to manifest spiritual life and power, as did our Lord. There is no other way to have a full manifestation of spirituality but through fasting and prayer, and there is, according to St. Paul, no other remedy for the groaning and suffering of creation than a complete manifestation of the children of God, as far as is possible here on earth.

Rom. 8:19-22: "The whole creation groaneth and travaileth in pain together until now, and waiteth for the manifestation of the sons of God, for the creature was made subject to vanity." Even the music of the birds is in a minor key. All animal life is groaning with unpleasant sound; there are sounds of discord, the wealing and wailing, barking and meowing, the howling and growling, all are a sign of sin and pain; the noise on the street, the clanging of the wheels on the street car, the sound of your automobile, the howling and whistling of the wind in windy weather, all these and much more remind us of the groaning of the creation. Why? It is because the sons of God, and more of the children of God, are not MANIFESTING. The crying of countless millions in Asia and Africa, the cries of starving multitudes that are dying all over the world after this second world war have reached a high, shrill pitch of suffering. It is all because the sons of God are not manifesting themselves. The cripples, the sick, the suffering, the insane asylums filled with the distressed, and hospitals running over with sick and wounded, the groanings of suffering humanity everywhere, all is because the sons of God do not have the vision, and know not how to manifest. The Laodicean, denominational, bound Church has so much riches, comfortable pews, stained-glass windows, but the CHRIST is left outside. Now He is knocking at the doors of a few individuals. Think of it, Jesus on the outside of His own church! The so-called Christians, and the makeshifts between Church and state, are of no avail as a remedy, and have actually become a reproach to Christ that prolongs the struggle and sufferings of millions. Under the sombre, leaden skies there is revealed to us a ray of hope! In the providence of God there is only one remedy that will terminate the groaning, instead of merely suppressing it as other agencies do. That remedy is the "manifestation of the sons of God." Our complete manifestation, of course, takes place when the Spirit quickens us, when "The adoption, to wit, the redemption of our body" (Rom. 8:24), occurs, but we have an "earnest expectation" available now, not for just a few individuals among the sons of God, but for the entire body of them. One can be a child of God all his life without "MANIFESTING" in this sense. Yes, one can even receive the Baptism of the Holy Spirit and not fully manifest. On the day of Pentecost the one-hundred-and-twenty received the Baptism and the fire, backed not only by days of real prayer, but as they were in the upper room *continually,* by many days of FASTING. The result—the world's greatest revival! It shook the whole city and countryside. These women and men who were in the upper room began to MANIFEST—AND SOMETHING HAPPENED. They were all of one accord, and their unity knew neither divisions nor sectarianism.

Most of the great revivals that have swept the land were born in fasting and prayer and can be traced back to that very thing. Some of the leading evan-

THEY ASKED MEAT FOR THEIR LUST.
THEY DID EAT AND WERE WELL FILLED,
GOD SLEW THE FATTEST OF THEM.
Ps. 78:18-33.

No. XII. THE GLUTTONS

The love of eating is "the second root of all evil." It is definitely pointed out by Christ as a last-day sign. Matt. 24:38; Lk. 21:34. There is nothing wrong with the enjoyment of "eating to live," but it is wrong to just "LIVE TO EAT." There is a big difference. Ps. 78:33 shows us plainly that this is the cause of sickness. More are destroyed from gluttony than from alcoholism.

gelists would prepare for the season of meetings ahead of time by a week or ten days of fasting and prayer. This accounted for the many healings and converts that they had.

Faith is not based upon sense-governed reason, nor upon the things of sight, but upon spiritual things seen only with the eye of faith. Faith deals with facts. The Holy Spirit seeks to have dominion of our body, soul and spirit. "Sense-governed reason," being carnal, is a stronghold which we must cast aside if we are to remove unbelief and have faith to fulfill God's great commission. On the battleground of our senses is waged the battle with unbelief. "Sense knowledge" is faith's worst enemy. It refuses to give the Word of God first place. In the fight for FAITH against unbelief, FASTING will so completely and effectually take control of our sense-reasoning that it is spiritually transformed into a different kind of reasoning. It becomes spiritual reasoning by faith in God's Spirit, through the renewing of our minds. (Romans 12:1). Even our natural imaginations are brought down. (See II Cor. 10:3-5). These are converted into Spiritual revelation, and power to believe with positive faith action. The spiritual warfare that fasting wages against our fleshly nature, explains why some dislike to fast and others seek to minimize its effectiveness. Fasting through the power of Jesus, leads us where sense-governed reason cannot walk. It is a walk by faith in the power of the Spirit.

SOME TESTIMONIALS OF FASTING AND PRAYER
BOY EVANGELIST

Little David was born in Phoenix, Arizona, Sept. 20, 1934. He sang his first song at two years of age. He prayed his first prayer at three years of age! At five Little David was about to go blind. He went on a three-day fast with prayer, going into the woods with some other little boys to pray. Satan talked to him and tried to discourage him the first day, but he kept praying and fasting. On the third day he went into the woods again and his prayer became more intense; the fast became prayer too. The windows of heaven opened and he received the Holy Spirit after the Bible pattern, and instantly he was completely healed and came home shouting! At the age of six he had another wonderful experience. At seven he was injured by a taxicab and again healed in answer to prayer. At nine years of age he was called to preach. At that age his spirit left the body and *for five hours Little David was in heaven;* a great light flashed in front of him, and he was called into the ministry. "Jesus told me to go, open my mouth, and He would fill it. I also received knowledge of many things that are going to come to pass," stated Little David.

At Age of Five, Little David Was Going Blind. He Fasted Three Days and Jesus Healed His Eyes.

There is much more to this remarkable story of Little David than appears on the surface. Let us go back before he was born. Little David's father, Brother Jack Walker, was not seeing souls saved; he became heavily burdened, crying out to God almost night and day, and still he was not satisfied. Then he undertook a fast in almost ceaseless agony and prayer for lost men and women. He received, from the sombre heavens above, a ray of hope, although he did not know what it was all about. This much he did know, and that was that God had answered his prayer. He felt that victory was his without a shadow of doubt. His fast and prayer lasted for fourteen days. *Immediately at the conclusion of this fast, a soul was given to the parents, and nine months later his son David was born.* This child evangelist was to do more than his father could ever do, and was very definitely given in answer to most fervent prayers and FASTING.

Child and women preachers are last-day signs that Bible prophecy is being fulfilled. See Joel 2:28.

40-DAY FAST TRANSFORMS LIFE

BEFORE

AFTER

FORTY
DAY
FASTING

"At the beginning of my 40-day fast I was proud, self-confident, and self-righteous.

"I thought I had *FAITH.*

"But the fortieth day of my forty-day fast, without food, I had learned more about God than during all the rest of my life without fasting."

J. A. Hida

J. A. Hida

Dear Doctor Hall:

Attached are pictures showing how I looked at the beginning and at the end of my forty-day fast without food (water only). The first picture seems to express self-confidence and pride, while the second shows a confidence in God along with a more humble spirit.

I was drawn closer to the Lord by this fast than I could have been in years without fasting. The experiences were so wonderful that I want to go on another one just as soon as I get my weight back.

What I believe to be the most important truth in Dr. Hall's books on fasting, is that prayer must be fervent and much of it combined with fasting, if one expects to have the best results. When I learned this, I began to really pray in earnest, and from that time on I have had no difficulty in praying. Fasting will help a person to be fervent in their prayers and receive answers to their hitherto unanswered prayers. Fasting makes prayer effective and reawakens our faith.

Fearful and unbelieving folk do not know what wonderful experiences they are missing in the prophet-length fast. If they knew, they would stop filling their stomachs right now, and start tasting the divine glories! My fast was near Christmas time.

On the tenth day of the fast I had a heavy pull of prayer like as of travail. After that, prayer came easy. Weakness left me the seventeenth day. I felt wonderful, both spiritually and physically after that. I had real anointing to give my testimony for Jesus. I have had more boldness, wisdom, and spiritual power than ever before.

We need a revival in the land and I believe one is underway now and it will continue to grow and grow if we can get more and more saints loosened up enough to fast and pray to get their lamps trimmed and burning. "As soon as Zion travailed, she brought forth her children." Isa. 66:8.

I was burdened for a spiritual reawakening in the East. I feel that fasting will bring revival.

Sincerely,
Jennings A. Hida
711 Willard St. Piqua, Ohio

For more details of Brother Hida's 40-day fast, write to him.

The weight that is lost is regained after the normal routine of eating is resumed. If a person was overweight before fasting, a few weeks after the fast he will be more nearly normal in weight, and if he continues to eat moderately, he will remain at almost normal weight. If the person was thin before fasting (and thin people, too, should fast and pray), he will put on weight after he begins to eat regularly again. In other words, protracted fasting normalizes the weight. Fasting also normalizes practically all functions of the human body as fasting is a law of nature ordained of God. Fasting is the greatest and quickest curative agent known to man. Fasting seems unreasonable to many. There is no valid reason why anyone has a right to condemn it. ONLY NARROW-MINDED PEOPLE CONDEMN SOMETHING THEY KNOW NOTHING ABOUT. No one has a right to condemn something that they have never tested and know little or nothing of.

WORKS BOTH WAYS: FAT PEOPLE LOSE WEIGHT; THIN PEOPLE GAIN!

Hermas, one of the church fathers, declares that the Lord appeared to him during a fast. Since the Lord is with us always, why should He not appear to those who will clear their eyes of doubt, bondage and unbelief with fasting and prayer? The fervent zeal of those who have declared they saw the Lord clearly indicates that their visions are genuine and not the product of mere hallucinations. Many Christians, after enforced fast brought on by illness, have claimed to have seen angels, their loved ones in glory, as well as the glories of heaven. The forced fast through illness, drew them closer to God; new faith was acquired and they were healed.

St. Thomas of Aquinas, probably the greatest theologian of the Roman Catholic Church, fasted often, seeking revelation of the truth. This was finally given to him so gloriously, that he refused to finish or add another word to the "Summa," a compendium of Roman Catholic theology, which was to be his masterpiece. When entreated by friends to finish the work, he refused, declaring that all he had written hitherto, was but "rubbish," compared to what was revealed to him. If every devout Roman Catholic would seek the truth as earnestly as did St. Thomas, with prayer and fasting, "Romanism" would soon be extinct, and the glory of the Lord would soon be in the midst of a reformed, spiritual Catholic church.

Brother Gayle Jackson, of Sisketon, Missouri, writes in his latest book, *"Divine Deliverance,"* the following testimony on the
EVANGELIST subject of fasting: "I was seeking God in fasting and
GAYLE JACKSON prayer for many days and nights. My weight was reduced from 200 to 175 pounds. During the time of my desperate seeking of God, . . . He planted faith into my heart so that it is impossible for me to doubt that my subject will get healed when I pray for them, as impossible as for me to try to blow out all the lights above our heads with one breath, . . . God spoke to me on the fourth day. He let me see a vision of the nine gifts . . . they would all be manifested in my ministry. On the ninth day of my fasting and prayer, God spoke out of heaven and said, 'Son, thy prayers are accepted of me.'"

After these fastings, Rev. Jackson's ministry has been greatly expanded. God has used Rev. Jackson to reach multitudes of souls for Christ and hundreds of folk have been healed and received the Holy Spirit.

Dale Hanson, William Branham, O. L. Jaggers, Louis Kaplan, Little David, Paul Cain, Tommy Hicks, Tommy Osborn, Louise Nankivell, along with hundreds of other ministers that have a definite sign gift ministry of the Holy Spirit, realize that fasting and prayer has an important place in all salvation-healing campaigns.

WORLD-WIDE FASTING-PRAYER CRUSADE
——— JANUARY 1946 ———

In 1946 a group of saints came together in San Diego, from various denominations, to hear the teaching of Jesus Christ's Gospel concerning prayer and fasting. Many of these Christians entered into consecration fasts. A real test was made as to the efficacy of fasting. Some of these fasts were from twenty-one to more than sixty days in continuous duration, without food. They were burdened to see the Lord move in a special spiritual way. These and many others wanted to see a world-wide revival for the salvation and healing of mankind and the restoration of the gifts of the Spirit.

The amazing results as these scores of Christians united in fasting and praying was stupendous! Many miracles of healing were performed by the
MIRACLES! Holy Spirit in the Name of Jesus. Demons were cast
ULCERS! CANCERS! out, lunatics healed, cancers disappeared, the blind saw,
LAME! BLIND! T.B.! the crippled walked, stomach ulcers disappeared, palsy was quieted, tuberculosis healed, asthma, bronchitis, the smoking and drinking habits were given up and many more sicknesses vanished. Scores of folk were baptized at the altars.

In this revival auditorium that the author was temporarily in charge of, we were privileged to see a thousand souls find Jesus that year. These converts were mostly service men from various parts of the nation. They also helped to carry the message across the seas.

A continuous chain of fasting, and all night prayer meetings conducted by Sister Helen Hall, went on for many months. She writes, "I went into 21

This is the most revealing sentence of this entire book. Here we find the true source of the stupendous power wielded by "Atomic Power with God."

days of fasting. In the next revival meeting after this fast, we saw over 3,000 souls saved. I could lay hands on the sick and they would recover, arthritis, T.B., etc." It was in the midst of these fasting prayer revivals that this volume was born. From then on *God burdened the author to launch a fasting and prayer crusade.* This soon became world-wide in scope. Evangelists Dale and Barbara Hanson, who were with us while this book was under preparation, also caught the vision. Soon many other ministers and spiritual saints of God became burdened to encourage and teach prayer and fasting in a greater way. Folk began fasting in Los Angeles and Southern California and then it spread throughout the west, and north into Canada. Folk began fasting and praying across the nation. Soon this most powerful message had gone throughout the world. Men and women travailed in the most powerful prayer prayed under the influence of a consecration fast. Such soul hunger and travail moved the hand of God and opened the windows of Heaven and God poured out His Spirit and Power in a mighty way.

Many calls, yes thousands of letters would pour in from all parts of the world asking for information on the deeper fastings, for truth that would take them deeper and deeper with the Lord and open the doors so they could have more of the Holy Spirit and His gifts. Even before "Atomic Power with God" was off the press, orders had come in for approximately five thousand copies, and requests for thousands of pieces of literature. This was a major financial problem, but our Lord supplied the need and members of the body of Jesus made it possible to print millions of tracts on a subject sadly neglected and overlooked, yet at our very finger tips.

Thousands of wonderful testimonies poured in from all over the world verifying the mighty power of fasting and prayer. They testified to all kinds of remarkable answers to fasting prayer: that the fasting type of prayer is far more effectual than ordinary prayer.

The author launched fasting and prayer revivals throughout the nation. Auditoriums were filled with crowds varying from a thousand to fourteen thousand. These were non-sectarian—for all churches. (See author's book, "The Fasting Prayer"—Price $2.00). This started thousands of people fasting and praying for a world-wide revival. This mighty tide of fasting preceded, and was a prelude to the major evangelistic healing campaigns that are stirring Christendom today, in which hundreds and even thousands are converted in a single campaign.

Dark clouds of doubts and unbelief had hovered over the church. Signs were not following believers as they should. Denominational barriers prevented the full working of the Spirit. Faith was without works, and was seemingly dead in many places. James 2:17: "Faith, if it hath not works is dead, being alone." Before there could be active faith in the body of

Christ, to produce "signs following," the dark clouds of unbelief had to be penetrated and removed. According to Jesus' teachings in the seventeenth chapter of Matthew, prayer and fasting was the remedy and the sure cure for unbelief.

CONCLUSION

We have prophesied a number of places in our writings: "A great spiritual awakening is in the making! A mighty revival of power, signs, wonders and miracles is coming! The operations of the Holy Spirit will move with greater power as more and more folk catch the vision and enter into prayers and fastings, as in days of old." Thousands of Christians have consequently gone into fasting from ten to forty days, all over the world, in behalf of a world-wide revival and more spiritual power.

Brother Wm. Branham in his healing meetings, led the way in proving to the world that Spiritual gifts could be exercised in a far greater manner than the average Christian had thought possible. Soon hundreds of other devout men and women who also received gifts of the Spirit were mightily used of God. Multitudes of sick folk having deafness, cancers, tuberculosis, ulcers, blindness, lameness, arthritis and scores of other dieases, many of which were incurable by man's power, were gloriously healed through FAITH in Christ's atonement. Many of the gifts of the Spirit are being stirred up in Holy Spirit filled people. As more men and women continue to fast and pray, more doubts and unbelief are being removed. There is more fellowship and harmony and greater unity.

We feel we are only in the beginning of the greatest revival the world has ever seen. Mighty miracles and operations of His Spirit will be manifested.

Praise the Lord; Jesus Christ is the same yesterday, today and forever. Let us all have signs following through fasting and prayer.

If you have not read the other volumes of this set, be sure to order and carefully read them. Many order extra books and help spread this truth among their friends. This is doing missionary work for Jesus, and being a blessing to the many hungry souls who so much need this fasting message. *"Withhold not good from them to whom it is due, when it is in the power of thine hand to do it."* Proverbs 3:27. Pass on to others the light you have received. Knowledge brings responsibility.

If you will mail in names and addresses of Christians, we will mail to them free literature.

See "FAITH TREATMENTS" by Author—Newest volume—written in 1952.

"OUR RAINBOW OF PROMISE," by Thelma Nickel—$1.00

CPSIA information can be obtained at www.ICGtesting.com
Printed in the USA
LVOW01s0251170415

434979LV00030B/504/P